CLASSIC MURDERS OF THE NO

Albert A. Thompson

Albert A. Thompson was born in South Shields, County Durham, in 1951, and has lived in the North East all his life. He has held a variety of jobs ranging from coalman to private investigator, and as a freelance journalist he specialises in true life stories. A crime buff and collector of crime books for many years, he began writing seriously five years ago and has since had many articles published in various magazines. The research for this book has taken him all over the North East, visiting many of the places where the murders he describes were committed.

True Crime Library
A Forum Press Book
by the Paperback Division of
Forum Design,
PO Box 158, London SE20 7QA

An Imprint of True Crime Library
© 1998 Forum Design
All rights reserved

Typeset by Techniset,
86 Market Street, Newton-le-Willows,
Merseyside, WA12 9BW

Printed and bound by
Acorn Web Offset Ltd.,
Normanton Industrial Estate,
Normanton, West Yorks WF6 ITW

ISBN 1 874358 23 0

CONTENTS

To Linda for all her help and encouragement...and for putting up with me in the first place. Also to Bella and Gareth, Tom and Chris; to Mark and Ronnie whose memory has never faded; and to the many people who have helped me during my research. And finally to Jeanette and Mike James of True Crime Library for publishing my first and successive stories and for their continued help along the way.

Ticket To The Gallows

The classic Dickman train murder case recalled in gripping detail

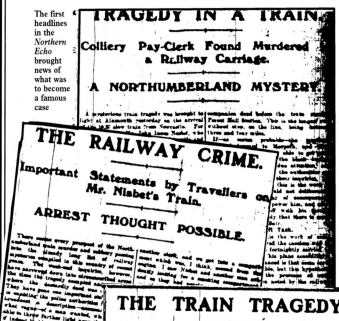

The first headlines in the *Northern Echo* brought news of what was to become a famous case

TRAGEDY IN A TRAIN

Colliery Pay-Clerk Found Murdered a Railway Carriage.

A NORTHUMBERLAND MYSTERY.

THE RAILWAY CRIME.

Important Statements by Travellers on Mr. Nisbet's Train.

ARREST THOUGHT POSSIBLE.

THE TRAIN TRAGEDY.

Man Detained at Newcastle in Connection with the Murder.

STATEMENT TO THE POLICE.

The money was always in coins, and for several years it had been John Innes Nisbet's job to deliver it, taking the wages to the colliery at Widdrington in Northumberland every other Friday, arriving in time for the miners on the morning shift to be paid as they returned from the coalface.

On Friday, March 18th, 1910, the sovereigns, half-sovereigns, silver and copper totalled £370 9s. 6d. Setting out from the Newcastle offices of the Stobswood Colliery Company where he was employed as a cashier, Nisbet collected the money from Lloyd's Bank, putting it in his black leather bag which he then locked, returning the key to his pocket.

Taking his watch from his waistcoat, he checked that he was in good time to catch the 10.27 train. Then he walked briskly to Newcastle's Central Station.

Newcastle Central Station (above and top right) where John Dickman was seen getting onto the Alnmouth train. Whether Dickman was with John Nisbet on the journey or not would later become a question of life or death

At the second stop at Heaton, where he lived, his wife Cicely was on the platform as usual to have a brief word with him. But when the train pulled in she was surprised to see that John wasn't in his customary compartment, but in one further forward. As she had a hurried word with him she saw that he was sharing the compartment with another man. She couldn't see this passenger clearly because he sat in a shadow and his coat collar was turned up, obscuring his face.

For 44-year-old John Nisbet, as his train steamed out of Heaton station his destination was still almost an hour away. The next stop was at Stannington, where two passengers alighted. They too were colliery cashiers. They both knew Nisbet by sight, and as they walked down the platform they noticed that he was still on the train. One of the two cashiers, Percy Hall, had seen Nisbet open a compartment door and board the train at Newcastle, followed by a companion, but as the train left Stannington the cashier couldn't see if the second man was still in Nisbet's compartment.

Six minutes later the train stopped at Morpeth, and a passenger got out and made his way to the barrier, where he produced a single third-class ticket from Newcastle to Stannington. "I think twopence ha'penny is the correct fare from Stannington," he told the collector, handing him the excess fare. Then he went on his way.

John Nisbet

A platelayer who boarded the train at Morpeth was later to recall glancing into Nisbet's compartment as he made his way along the train. It appeared to be empty.

John Nisbet didn't alight when the train reached Widdrington, and when it made its last but one stop at Alnmouth it was shunted to another line to allow a late-running express to pass. During this delay a porter walked along the platform, opening the door of each compartment as he made a routine check for discarded newspapers and the almost inevitable forgotten umbrella. There were no umbrellas this time, but there was something else: John Nisbet's corpse.

Every fortnight Nisbet took the train from Newcastle (above) carrying with him the cash to pay the mine workers' wages at Widdrington

Alerted by what looked like a trickle of blood on the floor of a compartment near the front of the train, the porter peered under the seats and saw the body. He stepped from the train and shouted to the guard, who with another porter dragged the dead cashier out from under the seat.

There was no mystery about what had killed him. The railwaymen saw only too clearly that he had been shot in the head. Five times in all, a post-mortem examination soon found. And his leather bag was missing, together with the £370. In addition to the blood on the compartment floor there was a small scrap of paper which no one thought significant at the time.

It didn't take long to establish that the shooting had taken place between Stannington and Morpeth. The killer had had six minutes to do his work, the time taken between the two stops. But was there more than one assassin? The bullets were of two different calibres, so it seemed that two guns had been used.

A reward of £100 was offered by Nisbet's employers for information leading to the conviction of the killer or killers. The man seen with the victim was described as "about 35 to 40 years of age, about five feet six inches tall, about 11 stone in weight; medium build; heavy, dark moustache; pale or sallow complexion; wore a light overcoat, down to his knees; black, hard felt hat; well-dressed and appeared to be fairly well-to-do."

Interviewing other passengers known to have been on the train, the detectives paid particular attention to the recollection of an elderly artist, Wilson Hepple. He said that as he was about to board the train at Newcastle he had seen a man whose description matched that of John Nisbet walking towards the front carriage. Walking alongside him was John Alexander Dickman, whom Hepple had known for at least 20 years. Dickman had formerly been a colliery company bookkeeper and cashier, like Nisbet. Now he was said to live on his wits.

Detective Inspector Andrew Tait found that whereas Nisbet's house was a modest one, Dickman's residence on Lily Avenue in Jesmond, Newcastle, was comparatively opulent.

Questioned at his home, Dickman confirmed that he had caught the same train as Nisbet, whom he said he knew by sight. He said he had seen Nisbet on the platform, but they had not shared a compartment.

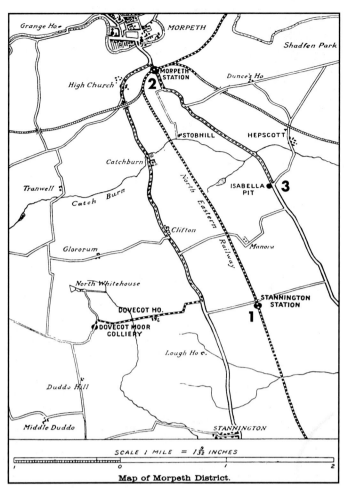

1. Where Nisbet was last seen alive. 2. Where the suspect got off the train. 3. The cash-bag was found here

making a good living through this and through other horse-racing ventures. But the discovery of a number of pawn tickets, one dated the day before Nisbet's death, suggested that the suspect had been having financial difficulties.

This appeared to be confirmed by further enquiries. In addition to giving a false name when he pawned various items, Dickman had been borrowing heavily, and just before the murder he and his wife had apparently been down to their last fiver. So where did the £17 come from? He said he had his own secret fund to finance his gambling, and the money found on him was the residue of that.

John Alexander Dickman appeared before magistrates on April 14th, and there was a short pause in the proceedings when Cecily Nisbet fainted. Nobody thought much of this at the time, because she was naturally under stress. But when she returned to the witness box at a further hearing a week later what she had to say caused a sensation.

She had fainted during her previous appearance in court, she said, because she had suddenly recognised the man in the dock as the person she had seen on the train with her husband!

Dickman added that he had travelled in a carriage at the rear of the train. He was going to Stannington to see a man named Hogg at Dovecot colliery, but it was the day of the Grand National, and as a racegoer he had been so absorbed in his newspaper that

Thousands lined the route to the Moot Hall where admission to the trial was by ticket only

he had missed his stop and had got off at Morpeth.

Beginning to walk back to Dovecot, he had felt unwell and had stretched himself out in a field until his illness passed off. Then he had returned to Morpeth, where he took the 1.40 p.m. train home.

Recalling that Dickman had been seen walking to the front of the train rather than the rear, as he now claimed, the detective was suspicious. Dickman was taken into custody and his pockets were found to contain £17 in gold.

Dickman claimed he travelled on to Morpeth (above) by mistake

"It is absurd for me to deny the charge, because it is absurd to make it," he protested. "I only say I absolutely deny it."

An officer was sent to fetch the two colliery cashiers who had seen Nisbet on the platform at Newcastle with another man. At an identity parade, however, only Percy Hall pointed to Dickman as the man he had seen with Nisbet. The other cashier couldn't pick out anyone.

Searching Dickman's home, the police also dug up his garden and even took his piano to pieces, but they found nothing incriminating. They learned that after leaving his job as a colliery cashier he had turned to gambling, apparently

While Dickman awaited trial further evidence came to light on June 9th. Colliery air-shafts were popular repositories for rubbish. Checking the bottom of such a shaft at the Isabella pit, a colliery manager found John Nisbet's black bag. A further search in its vicinity unearthed nearly a pound's worth of coppers.

The investigators learned that Dickman knew Peter Spooner, the colliery official who had made this discovery. Spooner had once told him of the trouble experienced in working the Isabella pit, which tended to flood. The mine was midway between Stannington and Morpeth, a few fields away from the railway and to the east of the track, whereas Dovecot – for which Dickman claimed he had headed – was on the west side of the railway.

Although no firearms were found at Dickman's home, it was discovered that under the name Fred Black he had used a shop in Newcastle run by a Miss Henrietta Hymen as an accommodation address. Items mailed to him there had included a gun sent by a firm of gunsmiths, and a revolver which the gunsmiths subsequently asked him to return as it had been sent in error.

Dickman hadn't collected the second parcel until about two months after it arrived the previous autumn, and when he picked it up Miss Hymen gave him a label to use when he returned the package. He was later to say that he sent it back without opening it.

Although Dickman hadn't seen Mr. Hogg at Dovecot Colliery on March 18th as he claimed he had intended, it was found that he had earlier paid Hogg several Friday visits. Were these trips dummy runs for Nisbet's murder? Had Dickman been checking the train's noise-level on the fast stretch between Stannington and Morpeth to assure himself that the racket would drown the sound of a shooting?

By the time his trial began at

The porter opened the carriage (left) at Alnmouth to see a trickle of blood on the floor

compartment of the first carriage."

"That is the last I saw of them because at that moment I turned round and walked in the opposite direction, and when I retraced my steps I found they had disappeared."

The colliery cashier Percy Hall was the next witness. He said that with a colleague named Spink he got into the second compartment of the first carriage. "After getting in and closing the door I went to the door and looked out of the window. I saw the deceased man and a companion coming towards me – they were eight or ten yards away. They came towards our compartment to get into the one immediately behind ours. Nisbet opened the door and got in first. I am certain it was Nisbet who opened the door. I had never

Above, the murder carriage where Nisbet was shot in the head five times and his body stuffed beneath a seat … Right, the murdered man's wife who identified John Dickman (left) as the man in the carriage with her husband

Newcastle Assizes on July 4th local feeling against him had become so inflamed that booing crowds lined his route by prison van from Newcastle's jail to the city's Moot Hall. Public opinion had already found him guilty.

A commercial traveller, Charles Raven, told the court that on March 18th he had been heading for platform four at Newcastle Central Station when

he was overtaken by Nisbet, with whom he was on nodding terms, and Dickman, whom he knew by sight. "I am quite sure it was them," he testified. "They went through the gate to number four platform."

The artist Wilson Hepple said he had secured his seat in the train's last but one carriage and was pacing up and down on the platform when he saw "Dickman

with a companion whom I did not notice very particularly, but I think he was of slight build. From their demeanour I think they were talking together. They were walking up the platform past where I was standing in the direction of the engine... I noticed Dickman and his companion were about to board the train. One of them had his hand upon the handle of a

seen the other man to my knowledge before."

The witness said that when he and Spink alighted at Stannington, as the train left the station he saw Nisbet looking out of his compartment's window and bowed to him.

Hall was then questioned by Mr. Tindal Atkinson KC, prosecuting, about the identity parade he had attended.

Police at the Isabella pit air-shaft where Nisbet's cash-bag was found by colliery worker Peter Spooner, pictured below far left

Police officers leaving the air-shaft after their search located just 19s. 1d.

"Did you point the accused out as the person you had seen?"

"No, not in that way."

"How did you point him out?"

"As being or very much resembling the companion of Nisbet, and I made one or two remarks at the same time...I said words to the effect that if I was assured that the murderer was in amongst those nine men I would have no hesitation in picking the prisoner out...I said that in my mind the prisoner very much resembled the party I saw on the eighteenth."

Questioned by Mr. E.A. Mitchell-Innes KC, defending, Hall denied that he had at first walked along the line of nine men two or three times, picking out no one. "I walked once," he said. But on being asked if he was prepared to swear to that, he replied, "I think not."

Although Hall had not seen if Nisbet's travelling companion was still in the compartment when the train left Stannington, the witness's fellow-cashier John Spink told the court that he had seen both men in the compartment as he stood on the platform at Stannington when the train drew away. "Mr. Nisbet was sitting facing the engine on the far side from the platform. He nodded to me and I nodded back to him. The other man was sitting facing the deceased, but I did not know who he was. He resembled the prisoner, but I could not swear it was him. There was nobody else in the compartment except these two people."

Questioned by the defence counsel, Spink agreed that he had been unable to identify Dickman on the identity parade.

Nisbet's widow then stepped into the witness box, where she was given a seat. She said that on March 18th, while she was having a few words with her husband as the train stood at Heaton station, "I noticed there was a man in the same compartment on the seat facing the engine at the far end. I only saw his profile. He had his collar turned up and he never moved. There was a shadow from the tunnel right on to the seat. The carriage was quite close to the tunnel just outside Heaton station, and although the shadow fell on the seat I saw his profile quite distinctly."

She went on to say that she had fainted while giving evidence at the committal hearing because "I recognised the man that I saw in the train – the profile again – in the same position. This was the first time I had seen his face exactly in the same position as I saw it on the morning of the eighteenth of March. Up to that time I had not been able to identify the man distinctly, but I am now certain that the man I saw in the carriage is the man I now see in the dock."

"You are more certain today than you ever were before the magistrates?" asked Mr. Mitchell-Innes.

"I am."

The defence counsel reminded her that at the committal hearing she had said, "All I can say is that he resembled the man."

Mrs. Nisbet replied that she did not recall saying that, and repeated that she had then been sure that Dickman was the man she had seen, just as she was now equally positive.

The ticket-collector at Morpeth station confirmed that he had collected an excess fare from a man who handed him a return ticket to Stannington, the stop prior to Morpeth, but he said: "I have not been able to identify the man, though the prisoner resembles him as much as anybody."

The foreman porter at Alnmouth station then told the court of his discovery of Nisbet's body in the third compartment of the first carriage: "The blood was coming from where his head lay... his spectacles were broken in two."

William Hogg testified that he was a contractor and at the time of the murder had been sinking a mine-shaft at Dovecot. He said that Dickman, whom he had known for nearly 10 years, had often visited him, but had not been expected on

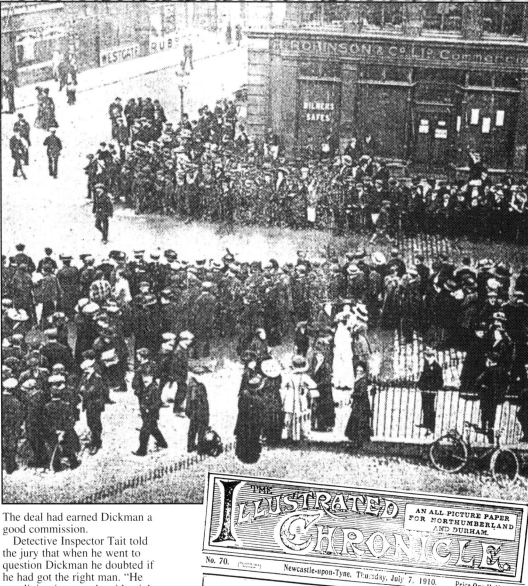

THE ILLUSTRATED CHRONICLE

AN ALL-PICTURE PAPER FOR NORTHUMBERLAND AND DURHAM.

No. 70.

Newcastle-upon-Tyne, Thursday, July 7, 1910.

Price One Halfpenny.

WAITING FOR DICKMAN.
A Photograph Showing the Extraordinary Interest in the Train Murder Trial.

Massive crowds lined the streets between Newcastle Prison and the Moot Hall

Henrietta Hymen told the court about the gun Dickman had been sent

March 18th, just as he had had no appointment when he called a fortnight earlier. They had a mutual business acquaintance – Frank Christie, who was helping to finance the work at Dovecot, and with whom Dickman had negotiated the sale of Morpeth Colliery some years earlier when Dickman was the Morpeth pit's secretary.

The deal had earned Dickman a good commission.

Detective Inspector Tait told the jury that when he went to question Dickman he doubted if he had got the right man. "He was living in a good residential district in a house costing forty pounds a year with rates. But inquiries revealed him to be very hard up."

Told that he had been seen with Nisbet on the morning of his murder, Dickman had said: "I booked at the ticket window with him and went by the same train, but I did not see him after the train left. I would have told the police if I had thought it would have done any good."

After a money-lender testified that Dickman had borrowed money from him and Frank Christie testified that he had financed a betting system which Dickman tried unsuccessfully to develop, John Alexander Dickman himself stepped into the witness box.

In response to questions from his defence counsel he said: "I said 'Good morning' to Nisbet in the ticket hall, but never saw him after that. I was never particularly intimate with him, he was just a casual acquaintance."

Asked about his finances, he said he had left his colliery post in 1906 after receiving a commission of £500. He had then inherited shares which he sold for £200, and he had subsequently lived by backing horses and placing bets for clients.

He said that on March 18th he had not needed to make an appointment to see Hogg at Dovecot because his friend was always pleased to see him, and after becoming engrossed in his newspaper and missing his stop at Stannington he did not realise where he was until the train rounded a sharp bend on the approach to Morpeth, where he alighted.

"Rather than wait for a train back to Stannington I set out to walk to Stannington as there was a coal drift I wanted to see anyway," he continued, saying that he had been asked about the drift's value.

But he had then suffered an attack of diarrhoea which in turn affected his piles, and he was compelled to lie down. Abandoning his intention to see Hogg, upon recovering he walked back to Morpeth and caught a train home.

He went on to say that at the identify parade, after Hall had walked along the line three or four times and then turned away, the cashier's path had been blocked in an intimidating manner by a policeman who seemed to be pressuring Hall to select someone, anyone, to give the officers something to do. "That is the impression I formed from the action of that particular officer," said Dickman.

Asked how well he had known Nisbet, he said he had known his name. He went on to say he had gone to see Hogg at Dovecot because he wished to know if Christie was contributing to the contractor's wages bill. "I wanted to know if Mr. Christie was bluffing me by saying he had no money."

Claiming that Wilson Hepple could have been mistaken in identifying him on the station platform, Dickman said, "He is not so young as he used to be...from my own knowledge I know it was all a mistake."

Dickman added that if he had seen Hepple he would have travelled with him. He said he believed there had been other passengers in the compartment in which he made his journey, but he hardly noticed them as he was so absorbed in his newspaper. He believed he was alone when he left the train. He knew nothing of the pit where Nisbet's bag had been found, and he had no recollection of Spooner ever mentioning it to him.

Questioned further about his finances, he agreed that he had been borrowing money, but said he had pawned some of his possessions solely to keep them safe from burglary.

In his final speech the prosecutor told the jury they had heard ample evidence that Dickman had been Nisbet's

Fascinating photographs of Dickman's trial shows an expert witness (above)

A rare photograph of Dickman in the dock at his trial

travelling companion. For the defence, Mr. Mitchell-Innes suggested that Hepple had been mistaken in identifying Dickman as the man he had seen with the victim. He also claimed that the two different types of bullet found at the crime scene suggested that Nisbet had been slain by two killers.

Retiring to consider their verdict shortly before 1 p.m. on the third day of the trial, the jury returned just after 3.30 and found John Alexander Dickman guilty.

"I can only repeat that I am entirely innocent of this cruel deed," he protested.

The judge, Lord Coleridge, thought otherwise, as he made clear in sentencing Dickman to death. "In your hungry lust for gold," he told the prisoner, "you had no pity upon the victim whom you slew, and it is only just that the nemesis of the law should overtake the author of the crime."

But although the evidence had convinced even Dickman's own brother of his guilt, there were many who had doubts. And when further facts came to light, the Home Secretary referred the case to the Court of Appeal. The defence had learned that Hall and Spink, waiting at the police station for the identity parade to be assembled, had been invited by an officer to take a look at Dickman, who was at that time in a room being interrogated. It had also emerged that Mrs. Nisbet had known Dickman by sight for several years, and had recalled seeing him quite recently, not long before her husband's murder. So why, the defence asked, hadn't she instantly recognised him when she had a clear view of his profile in the train?

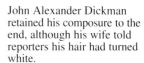

giving evidence, and above right, the jury listening intently to the evidence

John Alexander Dickman retained his composure to the end, although his wife told reporters his hair had turned white.

When the hangman John Ellis stepped forward to pinion him at Newcastle prison on Wednesday August 10th, 1910, Dickman asked him to wait a moment. "We don't wait at all," Ellis told him, but Dickman was only making the executioner's job easier for him. Removing his collar stud and putting it in his trouser pocket, he also took off his jacket, folded it and put it on his bed. "There," he said, "I shan't need that any more." Then he walked calmly to the scaffold.

By that time Dickman's defence counsel had at last become aware of the significance of that tiny scrap of paper found on the floor of the compartment in which John Nisbet made his last journey. It was now believed that only one gun had been used, Dickman wrapping paper round the cartridges of the smaller bullets to make them fit his revolver. **Either he couldn't afford enough ammunition of the correct calibre, or he had used different sized bullets to trick the investigators into suspecting two killers.**

Dickman was led from the door on the extreme right of the courtyard to the hanging shed on the left

In the condemned cell (above) Dickman and hangman Ellis (right) had a brief chat about clothes

The appeal was nevertheless dismissed, the judges believing the testimony of Hepple, Hall and Spink in preference to the evidence of Dickman who said the Lord Chief Justice "absolutely contradicts the recollection of all these three men."

Dickman's only hope now was a reprieve, and as the date of his execution drew near his supporters distributed handbills throughout London. "Must Dickman be hanged on Tuesday?" the handbills asked. "No! No! No! Wire the Home Secretary at once, and wash your hands of complicity in a legal crime."

There was no reprieve, but

"You had no pity upon the victim whom you slew," Lord Coleridge (right) told the prisoner

Within minutes of signing a petition for a reprieve, George Hunter shot and killed a man for throwing snowballs. We present the case of Richard Charlton, the killer whose death sentence was being campaigned against on the petition Hunter signed

GUN SIEGE ON A

CRAZED HUSBAND TERRORISE
A NEW BORN BABY

HOUSEWIVES in the village of Dinnington, a few miles from Newcastle Airport, may sometimes feel besieged by noise. More than a century ago, however, five Dinnington women experienced a very different siege. At stake was their lives ...

It would never have happened if Sarah Duxfield Fenwick had taken her family's advice. But Sarah was headstrong. And she was in love.

The romance had begun at a Dinnington barn dance. Richard Charlton, a local farm labourer, took one look at Sarah and decided this was the girl he would marry.

Sarah's family did their best to discourage the courtship. They didn't like Charlton, and they

suspected he was after her money: she had inherited £300 on the death of her father.

But the harder the Fenwicks tried to turn Sarah against her suitor, the more determined she became to marry him. The wedding took place secretly on May 12th, 1873. And as Sarah's family had forecast, the marriage was not a happy one.

Richard Charlton had a steady job. He was mild-mannered and no drunkard. But he was moody, and it wasn't long before the couple began to have heated rows, usually over money. If Sarah hoped things would improve when she became pregnant in 1874, she was to be disappointed. Charlton's verbal assaults now became physical.

Sarah's elder sister Ann had married William Robson, who farmed 268 acres on the outskirts of Dinnington, and it was to Ann that the troubled bride poured out her woes. Running their rented cottage, coping with a difficult husband and being pregnant, she said, was all too

much for her.

Ann had a solution. At her invitation, the couple moved to Robson's farm where Ann had prepared a room for them. Five days later Sarah gave birth to a son ... and on the same day, April 7th, 1875, Richard Charlton moved out and returned to his old cottage, alone.

Two months later Edwin Pye, an assistant at Wilson's, the Newcastle pawnbrokers, attended to a young man asking about revolvers for sale. Pye produced five, explained the merits of each, and finally sold one for £1 18s. The customer was Richard Charlton.

Shown how to load and use the weapon, he put it in a pocket of his grey tweed suit and departed. A few minutes later he was back, asking where he could get ammunition. Pye directed him to a gunsmith.

At 5 a.m. the next day, June 5th, 1875, William Robson was up early as usual at Gardener's House Farm.

Robson's labourers were starting to

14

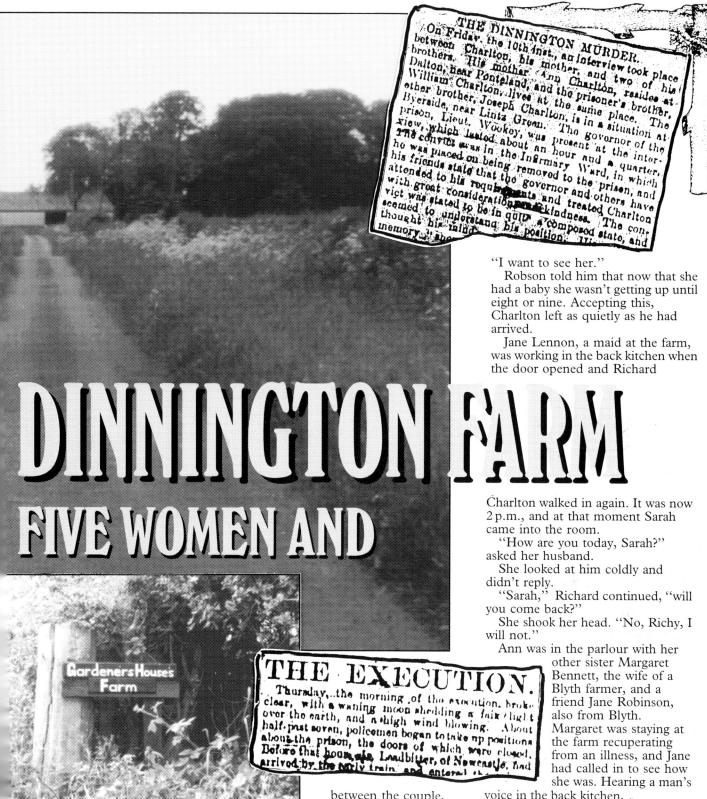

DINNINGTON FARM
FIVE WOMEN AND

"I want to see her."

Robson told him that now that she had a baby she wasn't getting up until eight or nine. Accepting this, Charlton left as quietly as he had arrived.

Jane Lennon, a maid at the farm, was working in the back kitchen when the door opened and Richard Charlton walked in again. It was now 2 p.m., and at that moment Sarah came into the room.

"How are you today, Sarah?" asked her husband.

She looked at him coldly and didn't reply.

"Sarah," Richard continued, "will you come back?"

She shook her head. "No, Richy, I will not."

Ann was in the parlour with her other sister Margaret Bennett, the wife of a Blyth farmer, and a friend Jane Robinson, also from Blyth. Margaret was staying at the farm recuperating from an illness, and Jane had called in to see how she was. Hearing a man's voice in the back kitchen, Ann went through to see who had come.

Her eyes widened when she saw Charlton confronting her sister.

"You have made this mischief," the husband told Ann, whose response was to ask Sarah to open the door for Richard to leave.

But it was the maid who snatched open the door, ran outside and took refuge in the barn. As she left the kitchen she saw Charlton grab Sarah's arm. Now, as she cowered in the barn, she heard first one gunshot

fetch the cows for milking, and he was sipping a cup of tea, when the kitchen door opened and he looked up in surprise to see Richard Charlton.

The caller looked tired. He had been up all night, brooding over his wife's absence and her parting words. She had told him she never wanted to see him again. Nevertheless, he'd decided, Sarah's place was with him at the cottage, and not at her sister's home.

Instead of making things better

between the couple, as Ann had hoped, the Charltons' stay had given Richard something else to grumble about. During their absence from their cottage, somebody had broken in and stolen some of their belongings. Richard had taken what was left to his mother's home for safe-keeping.

Now, determined to bring Sarah home, he set out at dawn and walked the mile to Gardener's House Farm, making for the kitchen where he saw a light.

Startled to see him so early, Robson asked what he wanted.

"Sarah," Richard replied simply.

15

and then another. She knew who was firing. She had seen Richard pull a revolver from his pocket.

In the kitchen, Sarah lay moaning on the floor, her head in a pool of blood mingled with brain-matter. Richard Charlton then turned his smoking revolver on Ann. She closed her eyes as there was a deafening bang and she felt a searing heat across her cheek. Then she turned and ran, grabbing Margaret who was coming in from the parlour. There was another shot as they dashed together into the pantry, and a bullet ploughed into the frame of the pantry door.

Slamming the door behind them, Ann bolted it, put her feet against it and grasped the sneck of the latch as Charlton tried to force his way in.

As they cowered in the pantry they heard him go away. All was quiet, and Sarah was close to death

Having no success with the latch, he pressed against the top of the door. It yielded about two inches, and the revolver's muzzle appeared through the gap, pointing downwards. The terrified women stood transfixed. There was a flash and a bullet struck Ann's thumb. But she still held onto the door.

After a moment's silence the women heard Charlton's footsteps retreating. Then they heard a movement outside the house. Guessing what her brother-in-law had in mind, Ann rushed to the other side of the pantry, grabbed the shutter and rammed it against the window. More footsteps were heard outside, and as the women listened the sounds faded away. Ann and Margaret remained in the pantry, crouching behind the door and too frightened to move.

Their flight to the pantry was witnessed by an astonished Mrs. Robinson who had just come into the back kitchen with Sarah's baby in her arms. Thinking Charlton might next turn on the child, she carried the baby out into the yard.

There she waited for a few minutes. All seemed quiet, and thinking Charlton had left she approached the house again, only to meet him coming round from the back, revolver in hand.

"Oh, what is this?" she cried.

Charlton looked at her blankly.

"Stand by, stand by," he said.

Dinnington — a village where two murders took place within a few weeks of one another

Jane Robinson fled through the garden and into a field with the baby.

Still crouching in the pantry, Ann and Margaret listened and waited. There was another shot and then silence. After a while, hearing no further sounds, the sisters inched the door open. Venturing out, Ann saw that there were now two bodies on the floor. Richard Charlton was lying beside his wife.

Ann and Margaret waited to see no more. They ran from the house, seeking the farmhands for help.

Bartholomew Watson had already been alerted. Hurrying to the house, he found Sarah still moaning as she lay in her blood on the kitchen floor alongside her husband, who had shot himself in the head.

Watson sent another labourer to fetch the police and a doctor. Then from the floor beside Charlton he picked up a five-chambered revolver. Four shots had been fired, and in the chamber one unused cartridge was left.

Mrs. Robinson returned ten minutes later, and with her help Watson carried Sarah to a sofa in the parlour. Then they brought a mattress to the back kitchen and put Charlton on it. Watson kept asking the victims if they could speak, but both were unconscious.

John Jameson, a Ponteland doctor, was preparing for his afternoon surgery when he was called to Gardener's House Farm. He arrived at about 3.30, and examined Sarah first. On the right of her head he saw the entry-hole of a bullet, but he could find no exit wound. She was beyond help, and all he could do was make her as comfortable as possible. For Sarah it was only a matter of time, he told Watson and Mrs. Robinson.

Richard Charlton was now regaining consciousness, and the doctor decided that he could be moved if necessary, although his head wound was so severe that Jameson couldn't hold out much hope for him.

Police found the bullet embedded in the pantry door-frame and another in the door about three feet up from the floor. Watson handed the officers 36 cartridges which he had found in Charlton's pockets, and the injured

The vicar was eager to give the killer a good character, but Judge Denham refused to let the witness go on

man was taken home with two constables to guard him. He was not expected to last the night.

Sarah Charlton died at 1.15 the following afternoon. At her inquest on June 7th, Dr. Jameson told the jury that he had attended a post mortem examination at which the 25-year-old housewife's death had been found to be due to blood flooding her brain as a result of her bullet wound. No other signs of violence had been found on her body and she had been in good health before the shooting.

"There can be little doubt in your minds," the coroner, Mr. I. Cockroft, told the jury, "that Mrs. Charlton's death was owed to the pistol shot which was fired at her by her husband, and that he did it deliberately."

The jury accordingly returned a verdict of wilful murder against Richard Charlton, still dangerously ill and under house arrest. Although now talking, he didn't ask about Sarah. Seven weeks later he was deemed fit enough to be moved to Morpeth Prison to await trial.

His first court appearance was before a Morpeth magistrate on September 8th, when he was allowed to sit throughout the hearing. His left side had been paralysed by his suicide bid, and he seemed to make no attempt to follow the proceedings.

"I never threatened my wife, sir," he said when asked if he had anything to say in response to the charge. "I was quite wrong in my mind at the time."

Three warders assisted him into the dock at Northumberland Assizes on December 2nd, when he pleaded not guilty to his wife's murder. His defence counsel relied on a plea of insanity coupled with evidence of Charlton's previous good character.

The vicar of Dinnington said he had known the prisoner for five years and had always found him to be sober, quiet and humane. Expanding on this view, the vicar added, "I have reason to know it is a correct one."

"That is your own opinion," said Mr. Justice Denham. "You have no right to tell us that."

Ann Robson told the court that Charlton lived about 20 minutes' walk away from her home.

"On the sixth of June, about two o'clock," she said, "I heard someone speaking in the back kitchen. I went to see who it was, and I saw Richard Charlton, the servant girl Jane Lennon, and my sister, the

deceased.

"The prisoner was standing opposite my sister. He took her by the right arm with his left hand and drew a revolver from his side pocket. He raised the revolver and fired. He put it close to her head a second time, fired and she fell.

"He caught me by my right arm and fired at the left side of my face. The ball did not strike me, but just the powder. I swung round, got clear and ran towards the pantry. My other sister was in the front kitchen and I helped her into the pantry ..."

Attempting to establish his client's insanity, Mr. Blackwell, the defence counsel, asked the jury to imagine that they were sitting not at the Assizes but at an inquest on Charlton as well as on his wife. In that situation, he asked, would they have had any hesitation in deciding that Charlton had killed his wife and then himself in a state of temporary insanity?

The jury nevertheless found

A row of what were once cottages, the one at the furthest end of the row being where the siege took place. The farmhouse (below) as it was in the 1870s. It has changed very little

Courtroom One in the Moot Hall as it looked in 1875 when Richard Charlton was tried there for murder

Richard Charlton guilty. Asked if he had anything to say before he was sentenced to death, he made no reply and stood impassively while the sentence was passed. Then, turning with great difficulty, he was helped down the steps to the cells below.

He was told that he was to be hanged on December 23rd. Morpeth had not had an execution for nearly 30 years, and his was to be the first to take place within Morpeth Prison – three earlier hangings which had been carried out at Morpeth since the prison was built had been public.

Meanwhile local sympathy for Richard Charlton was expressed in moves to obtain a reprieve. The mayor of Morpeth sent a petition direct to Queen Victoria, but it was unavailing. He was informed that Her Majesty was not prepared to intervene. This was the petition George Hunter signed outside Dinnington Church on the night of December 9th, 1875.

Charlton was visited by his tearful mother — from Dalton, near Ponteland — and his two brothers on December 17th. He told them that he could recall nothing of the shooting. All he could remember was his home being ransacked. Everything after that was a blank.

Promising to take care of the baby, one of his brothers assured him: "I'll look after him as if he was my own."

In an account of Charlton's health, the *Newcastle's Daily Journal* reported: "It may hardly appear credible, but it is nevertheless a fact, that he is less perturbed about his impending fate than multitudes are who never saw him. He is wonderfully well in body, being able to take daily walking exercise without assistance, except when going down or getting upstairs, in which position his paralysed leg of course fails him."

Charlton was mentally composed, understood his position and took comfort, the paper reported, from the belief that prior to the tragedy he had nothing with which to reproach himself.

As Morpeth Prison was surrounded by three hills, the governor's problem was finding a spot for the execution out of sight of the public. A spot near the prison chapel door was chosen, and there a pit was dug and a scaffold built.

Marwood the executioner duly arrived on December 22nd. Meanwhile Charlton had made his will, his assets comprising £10 in cash, his furniture and £240 which was being held at a Ponteland bank in Sarah's name. The money was to go to his brother Joseph, to help in the upkeep of the baby, Henry.

Then as Morpeth prepared for Christmas, 28-year-old Richard Charlton prepared to meet his executioner. The mayor had written to the prison governor, telling him that the bell in the old Morpeth clock tower would not be rung as had been customary at the time of previous executions. This had been decided by the council because "the tolling of the bell upon so melancholy an occasion would tend to shock the feelings of the community and do much harm to delicate and nervous people."

After a restless night, Richard Charlton awoke at 5.30 on December 23rd, 1875. He declined breakfast but had two cups of tea and appeared calm. By 7 a.m. crowds had begun to gather outside the prison, many would-be sightseers climbing the hills nearby for a view, at least, of the prison yard.

Just before the appointed hour of 8 a.m. the prison bell began tolling, and the prisoner, his arms pinioned by Marwood, walked slowly to the scaffold. It seems that his disability had been borne in mind, for he had only to mount one step nine inches high to gain the platform. Then everything moved quickly. It was all over before eight o'clock had ceased chiming.

It was a murder for connoisseurs of the curious, because in two respects it was probably unique. Whoever heard of a man signing a petition for a killer's reprieve and then within minutes becoming a murderer himself? And whoever heard of a man being shot dead for snowballing? Such things were beyond belief ... until the night of December 9th, 1875. It was then that truth became stranger than fiction in the village of Dinnington, near Newcastle

The trouble with 20-year-old William Wood was that he had never grown up. Although he was a miner at Dinnington colliery, he was still a child at heart, often behaving like a high-spirited 10-year-old.

The trouble with George Hunter was his short fuse. Aged 23, he too was a miner. He was also a bully prone to threatening anyone who crossed him. In his home village of Burradon, near Dinnington, folk treated him warily. George Hunter's threats had often been carried out. Nevertheless, he made friends quickly ... although he tended to lose them just as fast.

When George wasn't working he enjoyed nothing more than going out shooting with the friends he had made at Burradon colliery. His closest pal was Thomas Arnott, a fellow-miner who shared a cottage in Dinnington with the "Peter Pan" of the village, William Wood. It was to Arnott's home that George Hunter made his way after finishing work on the afternoon of December 9th.

He arrived shortly before 2 p.m. and after a quick cup of tea they decided to go shooting. Looking at the sky, George remarked that it might snow again, as it had the day before. On their way through the village they met Robert Schooler. He was also going shooting, so he joined them. The only one without a gun was William Wood. He'd been offered the use of Arnott's gun but had said he wasn't bothered — he'd only accompanied the rest as he had nothing better to do. He often tagged along with others in preference to staying at home alone and becoming bored.

The INCREDIBLE SNOWBALL MURDER

DREADFUL TRAGEDY AT DINNINGTON CHURCHYARD

Dinnington church, scene of extraordinary events on a snowy winter's evening in 1875 and marked to this day by a headstone (top right) engraved with a white circle depicting a snowball

Dinnington churchyard as it is today. William Wood's headstone is centre right

The White Swan, formerly the Carr Gate, where the pals were drinking before the tragedy

After shooting birds and rabbits with some success near Prestwick Lodge they set out to return to Dinnington as it was becoming dark. At Arnott's suggestion they decided to spend the evening at Carr Gate, a Dinnington inn, now named the White Swan.

By 8.30 they were merry, but not drunk William Wood seemed particularly lively. Every now and again he left his companions and went outside, returning a minute or two later, smiling.

When his friends asked what he was up to he said he'd been snowballing passers-by and urged them to join him.

"He's like a big bairn," said Schooler, and the rest laughed in agreement.

But Wood's antics were beginning to irritate the landlady. She had overheard what he'd told his friends, and beckoning him she told him to stay inside and keep quiet. Seeing that she meant what she said, he returned silently to his friends. She had no sense of humour, he complained.

"Oh, you wouldn't fire, Geordie!" yelled Wood, laughing at Hunter

At about 9.30 they decided they had drunk enough and set out to walk home, Arnott reloading his gun in case he spotted a rabbit which had been seen outside the pub. Schooler had earlier popped out and taken a shot at it, but had missed.

They were joined by another miner, Thomas Thorne, and as they walked down the street a snowball struck him on the back of the head. Thorne spun round to see Wood

The spot where William Wood fell mortally wounded

standing smiling at him.

"Pack it in," Thorne told him.

Ignoring the warning, Wood intensified his attack, forcing Thorne to run for cover.

Meanwhile Hunter was engrossed in telling his friends, for the umpteenth time, of his plans for giving up his job at the pit. He wanted to move away, he said. He fancied Australia.

His friends nodded sympathetically, recognising a pipe-dream when they heard one.

As they approached the church they met George Stokoe, the local schoolmaster. He'd been out gathering signatures for a petition to Queen Victoria, seeking a reprieve for Richard Charlton, who was under sentence of death in Morpeth Prison for murdering his wife.

After a short discussion they all signed the petition. Stokoe left them

outside the church, still debating the Charlton case. Thorne went on his way, together with Samson Mead, who had been in their company for most of the evening. Wood was still intent on throwing snowballs.

Arnott and Schooler were walking on ahead of Hunter and Wood when they heard Hunter shout at his companion, "If you don't stop heaving or clotting, I'll fire!"

Laughing, Wood replied: "Oh, you wouldn't fire, Geordie!"

More than 1,500 local people turned out for the victim's funeral

In court, Arnott was later to say: "About a minute or less afterwards I heard the report of a gun and we stopped and looked back. Hunter came up to us and said to me, 'Let's have your flask, Tom,' meaning my powder flask.

"I gave the flask to him and said, 'What have you fired at, Geordie?' and he replied, 'I have fired at Willie.'

I said, 'You don't mean to say you have fired at Willie Wood, Geordie?' and he said, 'I have, Tom.' I then said, 'Have you hit him?' and he said, 'Yes.'

"I left him standing and Schooler and I ran back to where Wood was lying on the ground with his face downwards, near the hedge adjoining the church. I put my arms around him and said, 'Are you hurt, Willie?' He never spoke ...

"I saw he was bleeding from his breast, and blood was running on the snow. I then left and went to Samson Mead's house, and he and his wife came to the door. Mead's wife and Schooler went for the police."

Arnott and Mead then ran back to

Arnott and a passer-by, Davison dragged him to the police house-cum-station, laying him on the floor and locking him in.

As Hunter smelt of drink the constable decided that at that stage it would not be proper to charge him. A search of the suspect's clothes revealed shooting items including two powder flasks, a spent cartridge, seven caps and 32 wads. When Davison subsequently charged him with Wood's murder, Hunter replied: "I can't mind anything about it."

The three miners, George Hunter, Thomas Arnott and William Wood, set out from Dinnington village (left) for an afternoon of shooting

After confirming that Wood was dead the doctor had the body taken to the Bay Horse Inn (above) to await further examination the following morning

Wood and found that Hunter was now lying beside him, his gun propped against the hedge. Arnott picked up the gun and handed it to Mead, saying, "Keep that gun, Sam, until somebody comes." He spoke to Hunter but received no reply. Moments later Police Constable Davison arrived.

Taking the gun from Mead, the constable put his finger in the muzzle. This told him that it had recently been fired. He than ordered Hunter to get up, but Hunter ignored him and said nothing, refusing to get to his feet and walk despite pleadings from his friends. So with the help of

Local children and their headmaster George Stokoe, who got the miners to sign the petition minutes before the murder

Dinnington colliery where Wood worked. Above right, the local gravedigger at the time of the murder. He would have dug Wood's grave

Meanwhile Dr. Allan Walker had arrived from Seaton Burn. After confirming that Wood was dead he had the body taken to the Bay Horse inn nearby to await further examination the following morning.

When this took place the doctor found 88 pellets in Wood's body. The victim's chest and left shoulder were riddled with holes. There was only one pellet in his heart, but three-quarters of his left lung was peppered with holes, and bones at the back of his left shoulder had been blasted away.

Wood's death, the doctor found, had been caused by shock coupled with severe blood-loss, and would have been almost instantaneous.

More than 1,500 turned out for the funeral, and a subscription was launched in the village to raise money for a headstone – still to be seen in the churchyard – engraved with a snowball as a reminder of how William Wood had died.

At the inquest on December 15th, Thomas Arnott said that he and Wood had shared a glass of whisky at Carr Gate inn on the night Wood died. They and their companions – with the exception of Schooler, who was teetotal – had also drunk a few pints of ale. There was no quarrelling and they had been sober and the best of friends when they left the pub.

This account of the evening was confirmed by Thomas Thorne who told the court they had drunk from

The victim had been stooping. And what harm could a snowball do?

one pint mug and a glass. After they left the pub there had been "a little snowballing, but just in frolic." About 15 minutes after he had returned home, Samson Mead came to his house and said Wood had been shot. Thorne said he was going to go out to the scene, but his wife and daughter stopped him.

Ruth Bell, who kept the Carr Gate inn, recalled that on the evening of December 9th Wood had been "very

lively." When she heard him tell his friends that he had been "pelting snow" she ticked him off and he was "very quiet after that."

Summing up, the coroner, Mr. L. M. Cockroft, told the jury that he thought it unlikely that Hunter's gun had gone off accidentally. After the shooting, he pointed out, Hunter had gone up to his companions and had spoken calmly. This would not have been the case if the shooting had been an accident.

The jury found that William Wood had been wilfully murdered by George Hunter.

The young miner's next appearance in court was before magistrates who heard evidence from a new witness: Christopher McDougal, a Dinnington mole-catcher.

McDougal said that he was about to leave his home on the night of the shooting when he saw someone throwing snowballs at Thomas Thorne. A few minutes later he heard someone shout, "Take a shot, you — !"

Another voice replied, "Geordie, you would not fire!"

Then there was the report of a gun, at a distance of about 25 yards from where he was standing.

Mr. J. E. Joel, defending, claimed that there were elements in the case which would justify the magistrates in reducing the charge to manslaughter or misadventure.

A different view was taken by the chairman of the bench, Mr. J. P. Mulcaster. Reminding Mr. Joel of a recent definition of murder made by Mr. Justice Denman, he said there appeared to be no extenuating circumstances to warrant a reduction in the charge. George Hunter was therefore committed to trial.

Pleading not guilty, he appeared before Baron Bramwell at Northumberland Assizes on March 8th, 1876. He was defended by Mr. Blackwell, a barrister with an unfortunate track record: every murder case he had defended he had lost.

Mr. Blackwell told the court that Hunter couldn't deny shooting Wood because he had no clear recollection of what had happened. But from what he could recall it had been an accident.

Mr. Greenhow, prosecuting, countered by telling the jury that if the shooting had been accidental, Hunter would have said so straight away. But he didn't.

Being snowballed was no excuse for committing murder, the prosecutor continued. The court had heard Dr. Walker say that Wood had been stooping when he was shot. Hunter had been in no danger — what harm could a snowball do?

Mr. Blackwell rose to point out that Hunter and Wood had been friends and there was no evidence of

Now Hunter was the subject of a petition for a reprieve

premeditation. Hunter's mind might have become clouded by the drink he had consumed, and it was possible that he had forgotten that his gun was loaded and that it had gone off accidentally while Wood was gathering snow.

Summing up, Baron Bramwell told the jury that if they decided that Hunter had wilfully aimed and fired at Wood, then they must find him guilty of murder, however much they might wish to reach a different verdict in such sad circumstances.

There was no evidence to show that Hunter didn't know his gun was loaded, but if the jury felt that his gun had gone off accidentally because of the careless way in which he was holding it — as his counsel had suggested — then he must be found guilty of manslaughter, the judge concluded.

After retiring for 45 minutes the jury returned to find George Hunter guilty of murder, but they coupled their verdict with a recommendation for mercy. Asked by the judge why they were making that recommendation, the foreman of the

Morpeth market square. George Hunter was hanged in the town's prison by William Marwood and there were reports that the execution had been a bungled affair

MARWOOD THE HANGMAN.

jury said that it was because of Hunter's previous good conduct and on account of the slight provocation he had received through Wood throwing or attempting to throw a snowball at him.

The trial had been a short one. Less than three hours after he had stepped into the dock, George Hunter was sentenced to death.

An ironic sequel followed at Morpeth Prison, where he was placed in the condemned cell. The execution pit which had only recently been dug for the hanging of Richard Charlton, whose petition for a reprieve Hunter had signed, was now re-excavated for Hunter himself.

The petition raised on Hunter's behalf by the villagers of Burradon was no more successful than that launched for Charlton, who had hanged. There was no reprieve for George Hunter. The authorities had learned that the previous good conduct attributed to him by the jury

at the end of his trial had been pure fiction.

It had emerged that the murder of Wood had not been the first occasion on which Hunter had shot at someone. In an earlier incident he had fired at two others, narrowly missing them, and had been warned by the police. And just a few days before Wood's death, Hunter had told someone else with whom he was arguing that he would shoot them if only he had his gun with him.

Now, in the course of a tearful prison visit from his family, he urged his two younger brothers not to turn out as he had. His advice to any young person, he said, was that they should learn to control their temper.

On March 28th, 1876, he awoke at 6 a.m. knowing that he had just two hours to live. Putting on the suit he had worn at his trial, he refused the offer of breakfast but accepted a cup of hot, sweet tea. His two warders tried to engage him in conversation to

take his mind off what was imminent, but he no longer had anything to say. Outside it was starting to snow, a reminder that but for the snowfall of the previous December he wouldn't be where he was now.

Pinioned by William Marwood the hangman, George Hunter went to the scaffold to become the last person to be executed at Morpeth Prison. At the inquest it was suggested that the execution had been bungled by Marwood, and that Hunter had suffered before dying on the rope. There was also a claim that one of the witnesses had fainted at what he saw. Naturally this was denied by both Marwood and the prison governor.

George Hunter was buried in the prison yard, his coffin end-to-end with that of Richard Charlton ... the killer whose petition he had signed just before firing the shot which was to lead to his joining him.

SARAH'S FATAL DOSE STRYCHNINE

JOHN BURNS had a pet name for 34-year-old Sarah Jane Holmes. He called her "Nancy." He moved in with her, bought her a ring and introduced her to his friends as his wife. Then he walked out, and that was more than she could take.

Her life had never been easy. Twelve years earlier she had split up with her husband. She'd kept in touch with their daughter, but the rift with her husband had been final.

She had known John Burns, a Newcastle solicitor's clerk, for about five years. They had been intimate for the past 18 months. He was a 33-year-old widower with a son aged eight, and in May 1883 he and the boy had gone to live with her.

A shopping centre now stands in North Shields where Sarah Jane lived at 38 Church Way, next-door to a pub, the Volunteer Arms. Her home was a cramped, ground-floor bed-sitting room, but Sarah Jane, her lover and the boy were happy enough there ... until the quarrels began.

The trouble was Sarah Jane's drinking. John Burns also enjoyed a drink — in moderation. But Sarah Jane didn't know when to stop. This led to increasingly angry scenes. In one of them she hurled a plate at her lover. It missed and hit the boy on his nose. Sarah Jane was immediately contrite: she had a genuine affection for the child.

In a later row, however, she called the boy a young bastard and put him out into the street. That was one scene too many for John Burns. He and his son couldn't go on living like this, he decided. So on March 9th, 1884, he and the boy left a distraught Sarah Jane and went to the home of John Burns's father in Coatesworth Road, Sunderland.

THE ALLEGED MURDER AT NORTH SHIELDS.

OPENING OF THE INQUEST.

Last night at about seven o'clock an inquest was opened in the Long Room of the Town Hall Buildings, Saville Street, North Shields, before Mr J. R. D. Lynn, Coroner for South Northumberland, on the body of John Holmes Burns, a child about 7 years of age, who, as stated in our yesterday's impression, died from the effects of a dose of poison alleged to have been administered by a woman named Sarah Jane Holmes on Monday night last, in a house in Church Way, North Shields.—The jury having been sworn, the first witness called was John Burns, solicitor's clerk, residing at Bishopwearmouth. He said the body just viewed by the coroner and jury was that of his son, John Holmes

Burns told Sarah Jane he would never return, but the pledge was short-lived. During the next two weeks he was often at her home, occasionally spending the night with her. This encouraged her to think that she hadn't lost him after all, but then he stopped coming.

Sarah Jane knew where to find him, however, and she began to harass him, begging him to return with his son. He said that her home wasn't a fit place to bring up a child, and he accused her of seeing other men, which she denied. Finally, he told her she could hardly manage to look after herself, let alone the boy.

In tears, she warned him: "If I suffer, he'll suffer as well."

John Burns dismissed this as a threat made in the heat of the moment. Sarah Jane loved his son, John Holmes Burns, and the boy returned her affection, calling her "Ma."

Burns had forgotten that shortly before his departure from Church Way he had complained of mice, and

The Volunteer Arms in Church Way, North Shields. Sarah Jane lived and committed murder at No. 38, right next door to the pub. The woman on the far right of this remarkable photo is Mary Mitchell, who fetched John Burns from the pub on that tragic day

he and Sarah Jane had gone to a chemist's for something to deal with the rodents. Since then Sarah Jane had visited two more chemists, signing the poison-register "Nancy Burns." Each packet she purchased contained enough strychnine to kill 10 people ...

On Sunday, April 6th, 1884, she met Burns again in the street. Tearfully, she told him she couldn't live without him, and asked him what he intended to do.

"Nothing," he replied, and went on his way.

Before he caught his train to Newcastle the next morning he walked his son part of the way to school and gave him two shillings to buy some books.

At about the same time Sarah Jane had a visitor: Sarah Ann Harrison, who lived in the same building, and who brought her a cup of tea. An hour later the two met again in Saville Street West. Thanking her friend again for the tea, Sarah Jane told her she was on her way to Sunderland to return an umbrella. She asked Sarah Harrison to accompany her, saying she would pay her fare and give her something for keeping her company.

The two then caught a train for Sunderland. They arrived at 11 a.m. and began the long walk from the station to Coatesworth Road. As they neared the home of John Burns's father, Sarah Jane pointed to the back door and asked her companion to keep an eye on it for anyone coming out, while she herself watched the front. It was lunch-time and it wasn't long before John Holmes Burns came out to play. Sarah Harrison saw her friend embrace him and take his hand.

The three then set out for the station, where Sarah Jane found they had missed their train and would have to wait for the next one.

"Where are you taking me, Ma?" asked the boy.

Sarah Jane told him they were going to see his father, and as an added treat they were going to have their picture taken in the market place.

Back in North Shields the two Sarahs parted company in Borough Road, Sarah Jane saying she was going to take the boy to see her uncle. This she did, leaving the child there while she went to catch another train. This time her destination was Newcastle, and at 5.30 p.m. she was

"Oh, Burns, I have done all this for you," Sarah Jane told her lover after she'd poisoned his child

standing outside the solicitors' office where John Burns was employed.

After waiting a while and seeing no sign of him, she went in and learned that he had left some time before. Realising that she must have just missed him, she went to the lodgings where he stayed during the week. He wasn't there either, so she returned to North Shields.

Later that evening Burns heard that she had been looking for him. He also received a message saying that his son was missing. Putting two and two together, he went to the station, and on arriving in North Shields he hurried to Sarah Jane's home.

Mrs. Elizabeth Mearns also lived at 38 Church Way, and at about 10.30 p.m. she saw John Burns hammering on Sarah Jane's door.

"Open the door, Nancy, and don't be silly!" he shouted. "I know you have Johnny in there!"

There was a pause as he waited for the door to open. Then he resumed his hammering. "If you don't open the door," he shouted, "I'll go to the police station and get a policeman to come and break it open!"

Mrs. Mearns decided it was time to intervene. She told Burns his son was all right. She had seen him with Sarah Jane in the Volunteer Arms only an hour ago.

Shaking his head, Burns muttered, "I don't know whether the boy is all right or not — she has threatened to do me an injury."

"Why don't you pop in next door," Mrs. Mearns suggested, "and I'll see if she will open the door for me."

Burns didn't take much persuading. He needed a drink. When he had gone into the Volunteer Arms Mrs. Mearns waited a moment and then knocked softly on Sarah Jane's door. "Mr. Burns wants to speak to you," she called.

From behind the locked door Sarah Jane replied that she didn't want to see him, adding: "Why don't you go away and mind your own business?"

Mrs. Mearns stood for a moment wondering what to do next. Then she took Sarah Jane's advice.

Shortly afterwards Mrs. Mary Mitchell approached, making her way home to Camden Street. As she neared Sarah Jane's home she was startled to see her standing outside in her nightdress. Sarah Jane asked if she would mind popping into the Volunteer Arms to see if Burns was there, and if he was to tell him she wanted a word with him.

Moments later, Mary Mitchell returned with John Burns.

"Oh, Burns, I have done all this for you!" Sarah Jane cried. Then she gasped, "I have taken poison!"

Burns caught her as she collapsed, and with Mary Mitchell he carried her inside, putting her at the foot of the bed on which his son was lying.

Johnny looked in a bad way too. "Oh, Da!" he cried when he saw his father. "I'm done! I'm dying!"

Sarah Jane, now sitting at the foot

of the bed, cried out for Mrs. Mearns, who rushed into the room. Meanwhile the boy kept repeating that he was dying. His back was now arched and he was struggling for breath.

"What have you taken, my pet?" asked Mrs. Mearns. "Has your ma given you anything?"

The child's mouth opened and closed as he tried to reply. "Yes," he at last croaked.

Mrs. Mearns turned to ask Sarah Jane what she had given the boy.

"He has taken half of what I have taken myself," Sarah Jane replied,

"and he'll share the same fate as myself."

Elizabeth Mearns ran to fetch a doctor. After hearing her account of what had happened, Dr. Tindle refused to turn out, telling her to find another physician.

Meanwhile little Johnny was asking for a drink — "But not the milk my ma gave me, it was bitter."

They were now joined by another neighbour. Hearing the commotion next door, John Davis, still dirty from sweeping chimneys, came in to see what was happening.

"Nancy has taken poison," Burns

26

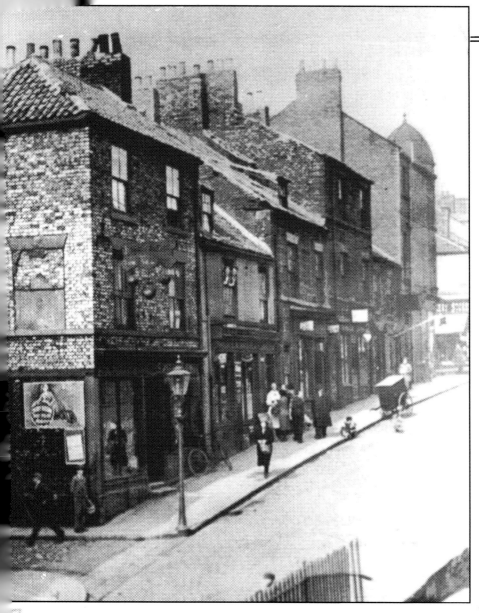

Above, Church Way, the street where Sarah Jane lived and where the Volunteer Arms was situated. Sadly, both were pulled down long ago and a shopping centre stands in their place. Left, North Shields railway station

told him. "And the boy has had a fainting fit with all the excitement."

Davis looked at the child, who was now writhing on the bed, his back arched, his fingernails digging into his palms.

"Good God, man," the sweep cried, "this boy's had poison!" He too then ran from the room to fetch a doctor, and he had better luck than Mrs. Mearns. In Saville Street West he found Dr. John Bates at home. Returning with Davis to Church Way, the physician saw at a glance that the boy was almost beyond help. He told Davis to fetch Dr. Gofton to attend to Sarah Jane while he himself did what he could for the child.

The boy was now convulsing, his back arching each time pain shot through his body. Dr. Bates tried unsuccessfully to open the child's mouth to give him medication. Fifteen minutes later John Holmes Burns was dead.

Dr. Gofton had arrived, and Dr. Bates now turned to assist him with the stomach pump that had been applied to Sarah Jane. The physicians left when it seemed that her crisis was over, and exhausted she slept on the bed.

John Burns remained with her, and at 4 a.m. she woke with a start and called for him. "I am dying," she said, "and I ask you to forgive me for what I have done."

"I will forgive you if the Lord will forgive you," Burns told her. "But you shouldn't have done that to a little child."

Making no reply, Sarah Jane relapsed into sleep. Earlier the police had been called as word spread of the poisoning. On their instructions Johnny's body had been removed to the Volunteer Arms. No more could be done that night, it was decided. If Sarah Jane's recovery continued she would be taken to the workhouse hospital to await questioning.

When an inquest on John Holmes Burns was opened the next day his father told the coroner that he had at first thought the child was simply shaking with fright. Burns said that when the boy said he was dying he had replied: "Nonsense, keep yourself still."

Burns testified that he had then asked his son if he had taken anything. The boy replied, "Yes." And Sarah Jane said: "We've taken it together."

Police searched her room without finding any trace of poison, and on April 16th Sarah Jane was arrested and taken to North Shields police station. She remained silent when she was charged with John Holmes Burns's murder, but when she was being placed in a cell she turned to Detective John Riddell and said, "I did not kill the boy."

When the adjourned inquest was resumed later that day she sat in the court staring blankly at the floor.

Sarah Harrison testified that the boy called Sarah Jane "Ma" and had willingly accompanied the two women when they found him outside his grandfather's home. She recalled that Sarah Jane had seemed "a bit distant" at the time — "it was as if she had something playing on her mind."

Describing his post-mortem examination of the child, Dr. Bates said that the body had still been rigid, the face red, the lungs and liver full of dark blood. The heart was contracted and an analysis of the stomach contents confirmed that death was due to strychnine poisoning.

Sarah Jane Holmes had also taken poison, said the doctor, but she had made a full recovery.

Two female warders supported her as the coroner's jury returned the verdict that she had murdered John Holmes Burns. Two days later, when she appeared before North Shields magistrates, she heard her former lover admit that he had given her a

"I will forgive you if the Lord will forgive you. But you shouldn't have done that to a little child..."

ring and had presented her to his friends as his wife. The day before the murder, he said, she had gone to see his father, telling him that they weren't married.

Burns agreed that she had been upset when he left her. He testified that she wasn't usually excitable. She had been ill only twice during the five years he had known her, he said, although she had recently complained of headaches. He denied knowing that she had been taking laudanum to help her sleep.

Sarah Jane Holmes was then committed for trial. Pleading not

Saville Street West. It was here that John Davis found Dr. Bates at home

guilty, she appeared before Mr. Justice Hawkins at Newcastle Assizes a week later.

John Burns told the court that he and Sarah Jane had lived together as man and wife since the previous May. He said that she appeared to be fond of his son, and she had been very sorry when she accidentally struck him with a plate.

On the day after the murder, he testified, she told him she had mixed the poison intending to frighten him. Then, while she was getting a drink of water, the boy had drunk some of the mixture she had prepared.

Under cross-examination, he said he could not marry her because her husband, from whom she had been separated for about 12 years, was still living.

Sarah Harrison testified that Sarah Jane had seemed very strange in her manner on the day she took the boy from outside his grandfather's home in Sunderland. The child had seemed

"... How you could take away this little life in the wretched way you did passes my compehension"

delighted to see her. When he asked where they were going, Sarah Jane had told him: "To see your da and have your portrait taken in the market, my darling."

Mr. Strachan, defending, said that Sarah Jane had loved the boy as if he were her own, and the poisoning had been a tragic accident while her mind was temporarily unbalanced.

He claimed that she had mixed

what was left of the vermin-killer with milk. She had done this before, and it had acted as an enema for her.

Concluding the case for the prosecution, Mr. T. Milvain recalled the testimony of the various witnesses, telling the jury that they had heard the particulars of as cold-blooded a murder as ever occupied the attention of a court of law.

Seated in the dock, Sarah Jane Holmes had wept throughout her seven-hour trial. She now heard her defence counsel tell the jury that if it had been her intention to murder John Holmes Burns she would more probably have thrown him and herself in front of the approaching train at Sunderland. Alternatively, she could have drowned herself in the Tyne while crossing the river on the ferry.

Mr. Strachan went on to remind the jury that they had heard a doctor testify that many people believed that milk was efficacious in staying the effects of poison. It was probable that Sarah Jane Holmes shared this notion.

"It could be that she mixed the poison with the milk with the intention of taking it to give Burns a fright, to try and get him to come back and live with her," the defence counsel continued. "Then, in going for a drink, the child snatched up the pot containing the poison and drank some of it, and when Sarah Jane returned from where the water was kept she drank what was left of it."

The jury didn't accept this scenario. After retiring for barely half an hour, they returned to find Sarah Jane Holmes guilty of murder, adding a recommendation for mercy.

"On what grounds?" asked the

judge.

"In consideration of all the circumstances which have led her to commit the crime," the jury's foreman replied.

Donning the black cap, Mr. Justice Hawkins told Sarah Jane Holmes: "Nobody who has listened to the evidence and paid attention to it would come honestly to the conclusion that any other verdict could have been arrived at on the part of those who had to determine your fate."

Going on to say that her cruelty passed his understanding, Mr. Justice Hawkins continued: "How a poor little child who had never given you cause for any offence — even though his father had — how, with him hanging onto you, kissing you, caressing you and going to your home and treating you as his tender and affectionate mother, how you could have found it in your heart, even for the sake of wreaking vengeance on one you hated, to take away this poor little life in the wretched, painful way you did, passes my comprehension."

The judge then passed the death sentence, adding that he would forward the jury's recommendation to the proper authorities.

Sarah Jane Holmes swayed in the dock and her sobs intensified as she was led away to await her execution, set for May 12th, 1884.

But her case had attracted influential sympathy. A local newspaper published a leading article

Sarah Jane swayed in the dock and her sobbing intensified as she was led away to await execution

headed "A plea for Sarah Jane Holmes" and a petition for a reprieve attracted 2,000 signatures. Sent to the Home Secretary, this was accompanied by a letter pointing out that the signatories included magistrates, town councillors and solicitors among whom were a deputy coroner and an official receiver.

The letter contended that the child had either consumed the poison while Sarah Jane Holmes's back was turned, or she had administered it in a fit of mental derangement precipitated by Burns's desertion and refusal to return.

On May 9th she was informed that her sentence had been commuted to penal servitude for life. When the prison governor brought her the news she sank to the floor of her cell, thanking God for sparing her life. Her daughter had visited her frequently, but her estranged husband had stayed away. And so had John Burns, although she had asked to see him.

MIDDLESTONE MOOR MURDER

Mother, Baby and Grandmother Shot Dead

SAMUEL WALTON loved his dog, his pint and playing fives. But the 31-year-old miner had less time for his wife Isabella and their baby daughter Esther Jane. At their home in the County Durham village of Middlestone Moor the couple seemed to have nothing but rows.

Walton's mother-in-law, Isabella Young, urged her daughter to leave him, but Isabella Walton insisted that she had married for better or worse, and it was her duty to stay.

By the summer of 1902, however, the marriage had so deteriorated that following yet another row, 26-year-old Isabella Walton made her move at last. On August 23rd she and her mother called on Police Constable Frederick Lambert. Isabella had left her husband, they told the policeman, but Walton had refused to let his wife take their baby. In fact Mrs. Walton's departure had not been entirely voluntary. At 10.30 p.m. her husband had put her out of the house and locked the door. The two women now asked the constable to go with them to the house to get the child.

Lambert accompanied them to the home, where Walton asked what he wanted. The constable requested him to let Mrs. Walton into the house to take her baby. Walton stood aside as Isabella and her mother collected Esther Jane and took her to Mrs. Young's home at 25 Albion Street.

After they had gone the constable asked Walton why he did not live happily with his wife.

"You don't know as much about them as I do, and you don't know what I have to put up with," Walton replied. Then, pointing in the direction of Albion Street, he told Lambert: "I am as sure to shoot those bloody bitches down there one of these days as you are standing here, and then I will give myself up to you."

Five days later he sold all his furniture and moved out to live partly with his parents, and partly with a friend, the son of a local publican. He also ceased reporting for work at the colliery, instead spending his time drinking and walking his dog.

Meanwhile Isabella took out a summons against him for persistent cruelty. The case was heard by Bishop Auckland magistrates on September 4th. Finding Walton guilty, they ordered him to pay his estranged wife ten shillings a week

A panoramic view of Durham city much as it was when Samuel Walton faced Durham Assizes under a charge of murder. He was not tried for the murder of his mother-in-law or baby daughter — only for the killing of his wife

maintenance, the first payment to be made on September 11th. They also awarded her custody of the child.

Walton now began further divesting himself of his possessions, a process that in retrospect turned out to be a countdown to tragedy.

On September 8th he gave his friend a bag containing his fives gear, and on the following day he gave another acquaintance a briar pipe, asking him to keep it for his sake.

On September 10th he walked the one and a half miles to Tudhoe Grange with his friend, the publican's son. They had a couple of sherries at the Commercial Hotel, and Walton then said he was popping out for a few minutes.

His destination, it later transpired, was the pawnbroker's shop next

He walked into a pawnshop and selected a revolver. Then when he paid his customary visit to the pub he showed his friends what he had bought, saying what he wanted it for

door, where he asked to see some revolvers. He was shown three, and selected one for which he paid ten shillings, also buying a box of 50 cartridges.

That evening, drinking with friends at the Mason's Arms in Westerton, he reached into his pocket and produced the revolver he had bought. "I have my first ten shillings to pay tomorrow," he said, "and I will likely pay it with this."

His companions told him not to be foolish and urged him to leave the country — nobody would know where he was, and he wouldn't have to pay. Walton replied that he was

his own master, and after a few more drinks he shook hands all round and left.

At about noon the following day he was seen crossing at the rear of his mother-in-law's home in Middlestone Moor. Knocking at the front door, he told his wife he had come to pay the ten shillings, but he wanted a receipt.

As he stepped inside, his mother-in-law turned to go upstairs for pen and paper. It was then that the killing began.

First Walton shot Mrs. Young in the head as she mounted the stairs. As she fell back to the floor he locked the door, turned to his baby daughter and shot her in the head. Then as his wife dashed to the back door to escape he went after her, grabbed her by the hair, dragged her back into the kitchen and shot her twice. The first bullet passed through the right hand she had raised to her face, the second struck her as she fell to the floor.

Struggling to her feet, however, Isabella ran from the house to the home of a neighbour, staggering through the kitchen and going upstairs to a bedroom. There she collapsed on the floor, blood pouring from wounds in each temple and in her hand.

Meanwhile another neighbour ran to fetch Constable Lambert, who on arriving looked through a window at 25 Albion Street and saw Walton inside with a revolver in his hand. Lambert motioned to him to put the gun down. Walton responded by pointing it at him, shouting: "Stand back, you bastard, or I'll shoot you!"

The constable withdrew and sent for assistance. As he waited for colleagues to arrive a bullet crashed through one of the windows of the Youngs' house, striking a wall on the other side of the street.

Two constables then arrived from Spennymoor and the three officers burst open the front door. Mrs. Young's body lay on the kitchen floor, and on the table was a revolver containing six empty cartridges.

Walton lay on his back on a

William Billington   John Billington

The following story, beginning on page 33, recalls the case of Thomas Nicholson who met briefly Samuel Walton on the gallows.

On the morning of December 16th, 1902, each waited in separate condemned cells for the arrival of hangmen William and John Billington, and both the condemned threw aside the levity they displayed before judge and jury at their trials. Each unhappy man was frequently visited by friends and relatives, but both were resigned to their fate.

The night before the execution was wild and stormy, and neither prisoner slept well. Nicholson, it was reported, lay on his bunk convulsivley twitching, but Walton lay still, silently contemplating the ceiling of his cell. They breakfasted on bread and tea but without much

A GRIM

Bishop Auckland was a popular shopping centre for collier families of the surrounding villages, and it was here at the magistrate's court that Isabella was awarded maintenance payments of ten shillings per week

certificate. Written on the back was what appeared to be his will: "His mother gets all. [Signed] Samuel Walton."

Isabella Young, 53, was dead, and Esther Jane, 11 months, died two hours later. But Isabella Walton and her husband were still alive. She was taken to Auckland Cottage Hospital, her husband to Durham Infirmary.

At the inquest on Isabella Young and Esther Jane Walton on September 16th, Dr. Anderson of Spennymoor said he had been on his way to Binchester when he heard of the tragedy. He went to the Albion Street home of the neighbour Isabella had taken refuge with.

feather mattress on the kitchen floor. His throat was cut from ear to ear, and at his right side lay his unconscious child, his arm tightly round her. A bloodstained table-knife lay nearby, and in Walton's pocket police found his marriage

Mrs. Walton had been laid on a bed upstairs, and on examining her he found she had a bullet wound in each temple. The wound on the left temple was scorched, indicating that the gun had been discharged very close to Mrs. Walton's head. The

wound on her right temple was caused by the bullet which had passed through the hand she had held to her face. She told the doctor her husband had fired at her twice, and as she was fit to be moved he had her taken to hospital.

He then went to the Youngs' home.

Samuel Walton was suffering from a throat wound which had penetrated his windpipe. The doctor stitched and dressed the wound and then sent him to hospital.

The following day Dr. Anderson carried out post-mortem examinations on both bodies. He found that Mrs. Young had been shot through her right eye, the bullet causing her death when it entered the base of her brain. Esther Jane had also died from brain injury inflicted when the bullet passed through her head.

A neighbour living opposite 25 Albion Street told the court that on looking across to the window of the Youngs' house on the day of the shooting she had seen a man's hand holding a revolver which was pointed at Mrs. Walton. She then heard a report, saw a flash, and Mrs. Walton disappeared. She afterwards heard three or four more shots and saw Walton near the window.

From Superintendent Daley the court heard that when Walton was quarrelling with his mother-in-law on July 23rd he had said he would swing for the lot of them.

COINCIDENCE

appetite. At around 7 a.m. the men were visited in turn by the prison chaplain, paying great attention to whatever spiritual comfort he could give them.

Reporters were admitted to the prison at 7.50 a.m. and noted that the wind was so strong that it threatened to extinguish the lamp in the execution chamber when the doors were opened onto the yard. Nicholson was given a drop of 6'10"; Walton a drop of 6'4".

Although securely pinioned, with their necks bared, the condemned men covered the

distance to the scaffold fairly steadily. Walton stared at the reporters but Nicholson never turned his head. The executioners lost no time in positioning them. Walton spoke the last words Nicholson would hear: "Good morning, lad. Keep thy heart up." By the time he had finished, hoods and nooses were in place. Curt nods were exchanged between the hangmen, and at 45 seconds to eight two men who had never met before became companions for the journey into the hereafter…

There are some interesting parallels between the two cases. Both Nicholson and Walton had been drinking in pubs named the Mason's Arms. Both were sentenced by the same judge within hours of each other and they were hanged side by side.

Walton had made no attempt to avoid being witnessed shooting his family – many of the neighbours saw him with the gun in his hand and heard the shots. And Isabella survived for days …

EGRAPH FRIDAY SEPTEMBER 12, 1902

THE BILL QUAY TRAGEDY.

At the Gateshead County Petty Sessions esterday, Superintendent Rutherford in ... the Bench that the police court ... proceedings against Thomas Nicholson, miner, who is ... the wilful ... murder of Mary ... ... and who ... already been committed for trial on a coroner's warrant, would probably not be taken for a fortnight. At any rate the ... could not be gone into that 'morn ... as no communication had as yet been ... ived from the public prosecutor. The ... he added, would in all likelihood ... time or ten hours, there were so many ... witnesses to examine. ' This announcement was ... great dis ... ... to the crowd of spectators ... had filled the public gallery of the court in the hope of seeing the accused man placed in the dock.

A DURHAM VILLAGE TRAGEDY.

A terrible tragedy was enacted at the mining village of Middlestone Moor, near Spennymoor, shortly after noon yesterday, when a miner named Sam Walton, aged 31, murdered his mother-in-law and his ten-month-old child, dangerously wounded his wife, and then attempted his own life by cutting his throat with a knife.

The motive for the grim outrage is

The Mason's Arms, Westerton, as it is now. In 1902 Samuel Walton showed his drinking companions the revolver he had bought at a local pawnshop — and was advised not to use it. By another small coincidence, Samuel Walton's scaffold companion, Thomas Nicholson, had also been drinking at a pub called the Mason's Arms shortly before committing murder …

The neighbour to whose home Isabella Walton had fled said she was on her doorstep when she heard two shots. A few minutes later Mrs. Walton staggered into her house by the back door, bleeding from wounds to her hand and head. The injured woman went upstairs, saying: "My mother is dead, baby is dead and I am dying."

Another neighbour said he had heard three shots fired in the Youngs' house, followed by a woman shouting, "Oh, my poor bairn!" On looking through the Youngs' window he had seen Walton with a revolver in his hand.

Arthur Edward Crow, a fitter living with his father at the Excelsior Hotel, Binchester Moor, told the court that he had been Walton's constant companion during the past few weeks. He described how Walton had produced a revolver at the Mason's Arms, saying he would probably make his first maintenance payment with it, and being told not to be so foolish. On the following morning, at about 9.30, Walton had come to the witness's home and had given him his dog, saying: "It's thine, lad, stick to it." That was the last Crow had seen of him.

The pawnbroker's assistant who had sold Walton the revolver said he had given his name as "Thomas Wilkinson, West Cornforth." It was a Belgian bulldog revolver with six chambers.

The jury returned a verdict of wilful murder, and Samuel Walton was committed for trial at the next Durham Assizes.

As far as Walton was concerned, the trial was a mere formality to endure prior to his inevitable hanging. He appeared indifferent to the proceedings

Two days later, Isabella Walton died in hospital from her injuries. But before her death, with a magistrate and the clerk to Auckland justices at her bedside, she made a statement:

"My husband on the eleventh day of September came into my mother's house. He said he came to pay me ten shillings. He said he wanted me to write it on a paper that I had received it. My mother went upstairs to seek some writing paper.

"She got on to the foot of the stairs and he fired a shot at her. She fell down and he fastened the door and locked it.

The baby was standing on the floor, and he fired another shot at the baby. Then he ran to the back door to get out, and got at me. He pulled me onto the floor by the back of the hair.

"He fired two shots and hit me at each side of the face, and another through the hand."

Dr. T. A. McCullagh, who attended Mrs. Walton in hospital, told the jury at her inquest that on making a post-mortem examination he found that at the right temple the bullet had not perforated the bone, but underneath there was a clot of blood on the surface of the brain.

The bullet entering the left temple had passed behind the eye, smashed the upper jaw and penetrated the back of the throat. Then it had disintegrated into small fragments, mixed with splintered bones. There was a small opening in an artery, which a splintered bone had ulcerated. Death was caused by a sudden haemorrhage from the artery. But for the presence of the splintered bone in the artery, said the doctor, he thought Mrs. Walton might have lived.

Once again, a verdict of wilful murder was returned against Samuel Walton. He had recovered sufficiently to appear before Bishop Auckland magistrates on October 7th. As he was still weak he was allowed to sit during the proceedings. Towards the end of the hearing he produced a piece of paper from his pocket, and when the chairman asked him what it was, Walton said it was his will, which he wished his brother to sign and a police sergeant to witness.

After permission for this was granted Walton was remanded in custody pending Durham Assizes. He told the court he might as well be hanged now.

Sturdily built, with close-cropped hair and a dark moustache, he pleaded "Not guilty" when he appeared at Durham Assizes on November 24th, charged with the three murders, although the prosecution proceeded only with the case of the murder of his wife.

A woman neighbour of the Youngs told the court that she had just left their house by the back door on the day of the shootings, when Walton entered at the front. She had reached her own doorstep when she heard three shots and Mrs. Walton cry, "Oh dear! Mother!"

Walton appeared to be indifferent to the proceedings as the evidence given earlier in the coroner's court was repeated. But his face brightened when Crow stepped into the witness box and described him as a good worker and a sober man prior to his trouble with his wife.

This testimony was supported by Constable Lambert, who under cross-examination said that he had known Walton for five years. The prisoner had been in regular employment, and although he had two convictions for drunkenness he was on the whole a sober person.

Mr. Mortimer, defending, told the jury that Walton had been contemplating suicide, not murder, when he bought the revolver. Had he had murder in mind when telling his friends of his first maintenance payment he would have said "I will

The condemned man's last wish was to be allowed to say goodbye to his dog. This was granted. Then he took his place with a child murderer on the gallows

likely pay *them* with this" (the revolver) and not "I will likely pay it with this." None of his friends had thought he intended murder.

The killings, Mr. Mortimer suggested, had been committed in a brief spasm of insanity by a "wild, uncontrollable lunatic" not responsible for his actions, or they had been perpetrated in the fury of a moment in which Walton was driven out of his senses.

In his summing up, however, Mr. Justice Channel said there was a great deal of evidence to show premeditation.

Without leaving the court, the jury found Samuel Walton guilty. In sentencing him to death the judge told him he could hold out no hope that the sentence would not be carried out.

Walton had nothing to say, and apparently unmoved, walked firmly down the steps from the dock between two warders.

Although a petition for a reprieve attracted 600 signatures, the Home Secretary announced that he could see no grounds for the sentence not being put into effect. But in the condemned cell Walton was granted a last wish when he asked permission to say goodbye to his dog.

Hangmen William and John Billington arrived at Durham Prison on December 15th to prepare for a double execution and next morning Samuel Walton and Thomas Nicholson were hanged.

The TRAGEDY BEHIND THE GRAVESTONE

The Bill Quay murder that led to Durham's double hanging

F ATE OFTEN hinges upon the apparently inconsequential. If a neighbour's baby hadn't woken in the middle of the night demanding to be fed, a young man on Tyneside might have got away with murder ...

The story began on Saturday, August 16th, 1902. James Stewart, a brickmaker and widower whose home was in the village of Bill Quay, near Gateshead, had gone to a cricket match at Hexham. He left his seven-year-old daughter Mary in the care of his mother with whom they both lived.

At about 6.45 that evening Mary was playing with her favourite doll at her home in Joel Terrace, together with her friend Johanna Scott. Then Mary's grandmother asked her if she would take a message to her Uncle Fred, who lived in Gosforth Terrace on the other side of waste land known as Hilly Fields. With her doll in one arm, Mary set out, accompanied by Johanna.

First they crossed the road from Joel Terrace to Cromwell Road. There they called at Christina Storey's house. Mary told Mrs. Storey that she was going to her uncle's on a message and asked her if there was anything she wanted fetched. Mrs. Storey thought for a moment, but had all she needed to last her over the weekend. Mary smiled, said goodbye, and Mrs. Storey watched as the little girl and her friend skipped up the street towards Hilly Fields.

The message was duly delivered and the two stayed a while with

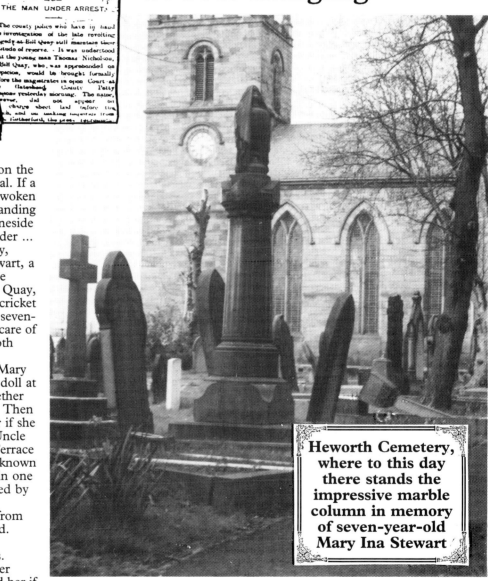

Heworth Cemetery, where to this day there stands the impressive marble column in memory of seven-year-old Mary Ina Stewart

Mary's uncle. Then at 7.30 Johanna said it was time they went home and Mary agreed. Johanna had to go in the opposite direction to Mary, but the two walked a little way together, accompanied by Fred Stewart. Then Mary set off across Hilly Fields on her walk home, which would take about ten minutes. Johanna and Fred Stewart watched her until

on reaching a hollow she turned, waved and disappeared from view.

At about that time 11-year-old Thomas Douglas was standing at the bottom of Jonadab Place, looking towards Hilly Fields, when he saw a man dressed in dark clothes pacing to and fro.

It was 10.30 when Mary's father returned home. His mother told him

33

that Mary had gone on an errand to his brother Fred and she hadn't come home yet. James Stewart was a little perturbed as he always insisted on Mary being home before dark, but he decided to wait a little longer as Fred wouldn't let Mary return alone at that time of night.

After a little while, however, he became anxious and set out to collect his daughter. On arriving at Fred's he was told that Mary had left for home at 7.30, Fred saying that he had watched her part of the way as she crossed Hilly Fields. The two now hurried to Joel Terrace, where there was still no sign of the child. Her father began knocking on neighbours' doors, asking them to help him look for her. All turned out and soon a large search party was scouring Hilly Fields, nearby quarries and a disused brickworks.

By daybreak on Sunday all that had been found was a shilling piece and three halfpennies, discovered in long grass in the yard at the brickworks. The search continued throughout the day, and on the Monday an exhausted James Stewart was resting at home before resuming the hunt when word came that Mary had been found. Her body lay with her doll in long grass near a fence in the brickworks yard, little more than 100 yards from her uncle's home. A medical examination established that she had been sexually assaulted and strangled. Oddly, a piece of uneaten bread was found in her mouth.

Superintendent Rutherford arrived from Gateshead police station and called Inspector Thompson from Felling to assist him. The inspector promptly began making house-to-house inquiries.

Bill Quay (above) at the time of Mary Stewart's brutal murder. Left is where Joel Terrace once stood. Mary and her friend left her home in the street to go across Hilly Fields on an errand for her grandmother

At the Swinburn Terrace home of James Dinning, a colliery joiner, Dinning's wife Christina said that her husband and a neighbour had gone for a drink at the Mason's Arms – 150 yards from the brickworks – in the late afternoon of the day Mary Stewart had disappeared. They had returned in the early evening. The neighbour was 23-year-old Thomas Nicholson who lived opposite the Dinning's, on the other side of Back Ann Street. He worked as a cartman for a local farmer, and Mrs. Dinning said she had later seen him on three separate occasions that night.

At about 7.30 she had noticed him come out of his house. He had been holding a piece of bread as he walked up the street. Two hours later she had been standing at her back door talking to a neighbour when Nicholson had come up Back Ann Street. He was wearing a dark suit and a white scarf, but no cap — which struck her as strange because

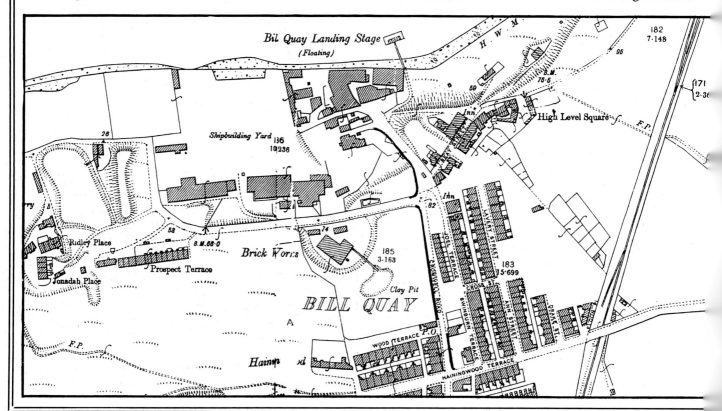

Children and adults in the streets of Bill Quay. The picture was taken in 1900, just two years before the ghastly murder

The first adjourned inquest was held at the Wardley Hotel. When it was reconvened at the Methodist Church, a coroner's jury found a local man guilty of Mary's murder

he usually wore one. He went into his house and came out again about 10 minutes later wearing brown corduroy trousers, with no coat or waistcoat. On seeing her he asked if her husband was in, and as she shook her head she saw Nicholson's parents come out of the house and approach him. He then accompanied them back inside.

At about 2.45 on the Sunday morning, Mrs. Dinning continued, she was woken by her baby crying and got up to make it a feed. As she was waiting for her kettle to heat up she glanced out of her window and again saw Nicholson. He was coming down steps that led into the back lane, and she saw no more of him because she had to attend to her baby.

Mrs. Morton, the neighbour to whom Mrs. Dinning had earlier been talking at her back door, confirmed that Nicholson had been wearing a dark suit and white scarf that evening but had later changed into brown corduroy trousers.

Another housewife told Inspector Thompson that she had been sitting

An 11-year-old boy was in Jonadab Place (above) when he saw a man pacing about on Hilly Fields, which can be seen to the left

on her doorstep at about 7.30 on the Saturday evening when she saw Nicholson coming from Hilly Fields. He was wearing a dark suit and was staggering as though he had been drinking. She had seen him go into his home and emerge a few minutes later when he went back towards Hilly Fields.

Mrs. Nichol, another neighbour, said that at around 8 p.m. on the Saturday she had seen a man coming from the direction of the Mason's Arms. Asked if she could identify the

man, she shook her head but described him as being of slender build and medium height. At the same time she saw Mary Stewart. The man spoke to the child before taking her hand and walking away.

By now Nicholson was the prime suspect. James Dinning had confirmed that he had accompanied Thomas Nicholson to the Mason's Arms, which they had left at 6.15 – he was sure of that because they had asked the landlord the time. Although Nicholson had drunk little more than a pint, he seemed unsteady on his feet. They had then gone to another pub where Dinning ordered a whisky but Nicholson had nothing.

Dinning said that while he was talking to a friend he noticed that Nicholson had disappeared. He stepped outside, saw Nicholson some 100 yards ahead and ran to catch up with him. They walked home in silence. Nicholson stepped into Dinning's house but stayed for only a few minutes before suddenly leaving. Dinning thought something was bothering his friend but didn't know what it was, and he later went across the road to ask him.

As he entered Nicholson's home he saw him pass through the kitchen and into another room without speaking. After a short chat with Nicholson's parents, said Dinning, he had returned to his own home.

Three witnesses told the police that they had seen Nicholson and Dinning near the Mason's Arms that evening. Neil Mackay, who had known Nicholson all his life, said that on the Saturday night he had been standing at the end of Haywood Terrace when he saw Nicholson approaching. Asked where he was going, Nicholson said he might go to Felling or he might go to Gateshead to buy himself a suit. Seeing that he seemed drunk, Mackay advised him to go home. Nicholson's response was to strike a wall with his fist, saying he was all right. Mackay then saw him start to cross Hilly Fields. He noticed no one else about at the time.

On Tuesday, August 19th, Inspector Thompson went to Nicholson's home to arrest him. Asked to account for his movements after 6 p.m. on the Saturday night, Nicholson said: "I went over to Ed Shell's house [the Mason's Arms] and remained there until closing time."

The inspector had already questioned Shell, who told him that Nicholson had arrived with Dinning at about 5 p.m. and left at 6.15, when he asked him the time. Nicholson had not returned again that night.

Nicholson was now asked: "Where is the suit of clothes you were wearing on Saturday night?"

He turned to his mother, who had remained silent throughout the interview. "Where are they, Mother?" he asked.

"In Lightfoot's pawn shop," she replied.

"Were you anywhere near Hilly Fields on Saturday night?" the inspector asked Nicholson.

"I only crossed them to get to the Mason's," he answered.

Charged with the wilful murder of Mary Ina Stewart, he made no reply but hung his head.

On August 21st the funeral was held. Crowds that had gathered from early morning lined the pavement and the hymn, "Shall we gather at the river?" was sung openly by the people. James Stewart, Mary's father, stood at his front door, head bowed, with tears running down his face. The route from Bill Quay to the cemetery at Heworth was crowded, but the blinds and curtains in all the houses were drawn shut. Many of Mary's school friends and her teachers attended the burial.

The original inquest hearing held at the Wardley Hotel had been adjourned on August 18th. When it was reconvened at the Methodist Church in Bill Quay on September 9th, the court heard from the Durham county analyst that bloodstains had been found on a jacket, shirt and trousers belonging to Nicholson, but there were no traces of semen. Blood had also been found on Mary Stewart's underwear and on her two petticoats.

James Dinning told the court that on the day following Mary's disappearance he had gone to Nicholson's home and asked him where he had been the previous evening when not in his company.

It was believed that the body had been carried to the spot where it was found

Nicholson had hardly spoken to him.

Dr. J. Mackay said that on completing a post-mortem examination he had concluded that Mary Stewart had died from suffocation, loss of blood and shock consistent with injuries received in her genital area. She had puncture wounds to her head, arm and shin, inflicted by a blunt instrument after her death, or after she had lost a lot of blood.

As there was little blood where her body lay, he believed she had been killed elsewhere and carried to the spot where she was found. She had been discovered lying on her back in a position facilitating the insertion of a male organ, an act consistent with injuries found in her genital region.

After retiring for 20 minutes the coroner's jury returned a unanimous verdict that Mary Ina Stewart had been wilfully murdered by Thomas Nicholson.

When his trial at Durham Assizes began on November 26th, 1902, he looked cheerful, pleaded "not guilty" in a firm voice and smiled throughout the proceedings.

Mr. Joel, prosecuting, told the jury that one point which they would have to weigh carefully was that Nicholson had been seen at 3 a.m. on the night of the murder, coming out from his back door fully dressed.

"Had he any purpose in going outside at that time of the morning?" asked the prosecutor. "Was there any purpose which in connection with the

He saw it as a joke and was beaming when he was sentenced to death

other circumstances of the tragedy might lead him to leave his house at three o'clock in the morning?"

Mr. Joel went on to say that the clothes Nicholson had worn on the Saturday night of the murder had been pawned between 9 a.m. and 10 a.m. on the following Monday. "Were the bloodstains found on them the result of his phantom nose-bleeds that he has alleged he had, but no one has ever seen, or something else?"

For the defence, Mr. Mitchell Innes pointed out that Hilly Fields had many hollows where a man could conceal himself without difficulty.

Cross-examining Mrs. Nichols — who said she had seen Mary Stewart with a man of similar build to Nicholson — Mr. Mitchell Innes asked: "Is it not a fact that you were taken to the exercise yard at Durham Prison where a few men were walking, and you were asked to point out the person whom you saw that night?"

Mrs. Nichol nodded.

"Is it not a fact that you picked out someone clearly different in build and appearance to Nicholson?"

"I picked him out because of his dress," said Mrs. Nichol.

The prison governor confirmed that she had picked out a man six inches shorter than Nicholson.

Summing up, Mr. Justice Channell told the jury that he believed the strongest evidence against Nicholson was that he had changed his trousers on the night of the murder and could not explain why.

After deliberating for just over half an hour the jury found Thomas

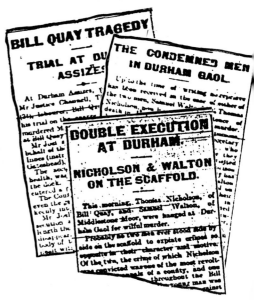

Nicholson guilty. As he was sentenced to death he wasn't merely smiling: he was beaming! He seemed to regard it all as a joke, and continued to appear carefree when his parents visited him in prison. His manner changed only when his execution was imminent and he realised at last that there was to be no reprieve. There had been no petition for mercy: the people of Bill Quay no longer had any time for him.

But at least he was not without company on the gallows at Durham Gaol on 16th December, 1902.

Revenge Is Sweet ...
POLICEMAN SHOOTS POLICEMAN

Former Sergeant Commits Cold-Blooded Murder In A Durham Street

EVERYTHING WAS going according to plan. Joseph Scott was 12 when he decided to be a policeman. At 20 he became one. His elder brother was already in the force and gaining promotion. Joseph promised he would catch him up, and he did. Within 25 years both were County Durham superintendents, Joseph at Jarrow, his brother Percival at Castle Eden.

Joseph was now 45. His sights were set on becoming a chief constable, and it seemed that it would be only a matter of time before he fulfilled his ambition. His career had been that of a model policeman, and he had no regrets.

True, he'd had to dismiss officers from the force from time to time, and that was something he never enjoyed. But it was part of the job, and a step taken only when there was no alternative — as in the case of an officer who had shot

DREADFUL TRAGEDY IN THIS CITY.
A SUPERINTENDENT OF POLICE SHOT.
SUICIDE OF THE MURDERER
Certainly the most tragic event which has occurred within the ancient city of Durham ... ... at least a quarter ...

SHOCKING MURDER
OF
SUPERINTENDENT SCOTT
OF JARROW.
—
DOUBLE TRAGEDY AT DURHAM.
—
THE MURDERER SHOOTS HIMSELF.

SUPT. SCOTT, OF JARROW, SHOT DEAD.
A telegram was received in Jarrow this morning, stating that Superintendent Scott had been shot dead by an ex-sergeant late of Hebburn. News has caused a painful sensation in ... The magistrates and police were in the court when the telegram arrived. ... ceased leaves a widow and children.
—
MR BRIGHT'S HEALTH.
Telegram from Rochdale to the Press Association.

a colleague and who committed suicide after he was dismissed.

On the last day of each month Superintendent Scott went to Durham to collect his men's wages. May 31st, 1888, was no exception. The superintendent had spent the previous day prosecuting at

Jarrow Magistrates' Court. The defendants had included John Fannen, a miner who lived in Hebburn. Unable to pay his fine, Fannen was to be sent to Durham Prison. As Superintendent Scott was going to Durham the next day, he agreed to act as the prisoner's escort. He'd not lost a prisoner yet, the imposing, six-foot-three officer had often remarked, and he enjoyed his trips to Durham where he would meet his fellow-superintendents and swap gossip.

Thursday, May 31st, began brightly as Scott and his prisoner boarded the train at South Shields for Newcastle, where they would change trains to proceed to Durham.

Someone else also rose early that morning. Benjamin Wright was up and about by 5 a.m. His wife and four children were still sleeping soundly when he closed the door quietly behind him and set out from his cottage in the village of Herrington. But he wasn't unobserved. A woman walking through the village with her nephew saw him at about 6.30. He looked preoccupied, and the woman watched him for a few moments, wondering if he was planning another of his jaunts. He often took villagers with him to the top of the church tower, the highest point in the village, to show them the view for miles around through his telescope.

But it wasn't a telescope that Wright was carrying today. One pocket held a revolver, and a rifle was concealed under his coat.

At about 8.30 a.m. Constable Friar was on duty in Sunderland when he saw Wright whom he knew as a former colleague. The officer stopped to ask if all was well with him. Wright looked at him but said nothing. He seemed confused and Friar repeated his question. Again there was no answer and Wright pushed past him.

This seemed odd, thought the constable, but he had other matters to attend to, so he let Wright go on his way.

If PC Friar had received an answer to his question he might have learned that all was far from well with Benjamin Wright. Now 48, he had left his job as a labourer three weeks previously and was unemployed.

His 16-year career as a policeman had begun promisingly. Like Joseph Scott, he had been ambitious. Hoping to become an inspector, he had been commended as conscientious, the smartest man at his station and a credit to the force. But although his superiors thought well of him, his fellow-constables found him surly, overbearing and unwilling to be drawn into conversation, preferring to keep himself to himself. At the same time, however, he was an active member of the Wesleyan Church and the Police Christian Association.

By 1882 he was a sergeant, but four years later he began to cause concern. He started drinking heavily and failed to obey orders. By June 1887 reports of Wright's behaviour had reached Superintendent Scott, who reduced him from sergeant to constable and transferred him to Darlington.

The problem policeman pleaded in vain for another chance. Scott pointed out that he had already been given several opportunities to come into line but had failed to respond.

At Darlington the embittered constable had

refused to obey any orders, and in August 1887 he was dismissed from the force.

Two hours after Benjamin Wright's encounter with PC Friar in Sunderland, Superintendent Scott and his prisoner arrived at Durham railway station. The sun was still shining as they set off down North Road, John Fannen handcuffed to his escort.

At the Neville Hotel on North Road a barmaid was polishing tables in the bar when she heard the bell ring for service in the parlour. On responding she found a man in the parlour whom she would later identify as Benjamin Wright. He was leaning on a table, looking out of the window. As she entered the parlour he glanced at the clock on the wall and asked her to bring him a glass of whisky.

When she returned she found he had moved closer to the window and was looking towards the railway station. He seemed to be waiting for someone.

Fumbling in his pocket, he produced a revolver and put it in his mouth ...

"It's very sunny today," said the barmaid to make conversation, but the customer made it clear that he'd no wish to talk. Sensing she wasn't wanted, the barmaid returned to the bar and resumed polishing the tables. About half an hour later she heard the door slam behind the customer in the parlour as he left.

Meanwhile Superintendent Scott and his prisoner Fannen had reached the bottom of North Road and crossed Framwellgate Bridge. Durham

The foreground of this 1890s view of the city of Durham shows Framwellgate. Superintendent Scott and his prisoner were halfway up Silver Street here when the gunman struck ...

Prison was about 10 minutes' walk away as they turned left into Silver Street. Fannen was on Scott's left, and in his right hand the superintendent carried the bag which was to hold the wages.

They were about halfway up the street when Fannen became aware of a smartly dressed man coming up quickly behind them. Fannen turned slightly, but Scott took no notice.

Fannen thought the man was going to tap the superintendent on the shoulder to attract his attention. Then he heard a loud bang and Scott collapsed.

Benjamin Wright stepped back, smiling as he looked at the superintendent lying motionless. Fumbling in his pocket, he produced a revolver, placed its barrel in his mouth and pulled the trigger. There was a second report and he too fell to the ground, a few feet from where

Scott lay dying.

Stunned by the swiftness and horror of the events, Fannen lifted the superintendent's head, urging him to say something. A pool of blood was forming, some of it soaking the prisoner's trousers as he tried to stem the flow from the stricken policeman.

Escape was now possible for Fannen, but it hadn't occurred to him. He was too busy trying to help the superintendent as a crowd gathered and someone was sent to fetch police assistance.

The messenger ran to the nearby police courts where he blurted out what had happened. A stunned Chief Constable John Smith and the Mayor of Durham, Alderman W. Blackett, rushed to the scene accompanied by several constables.

Dr. Mason Vann, Durham's police surgeon, was walking up Silver Street when he saw the

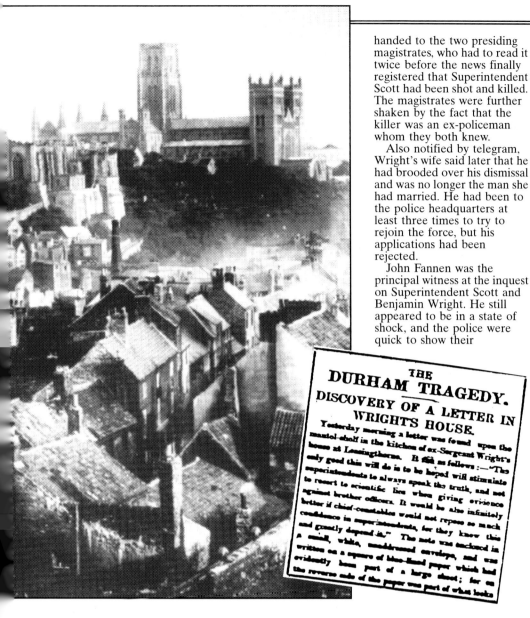

handed to the two presiding magistrates, who had to read it twice before the news finally registered that Superintendent Scott had been shot and killed. The magistrates were further shaken by the fact that the killer was an ex-policeman whom they both knew.

Also notified by telegram, Wright's wife said later that he had brooded over his dismissal and was no longer the man she had married. He had been to the police headquarters at least three times to try to rejoin the force, but his applications had been rejected.

John Fannen was the principal witness at the inquest on Superintendent Scott and Benjamin Wright. He still appeared to be in a state of shock, and the police were quick to show their

against his former superior officer, and this feeling had developed into something akin to madness. But there had been a strong element of premeditation in the killing. As an ex-policeman Wright knew that Scott would be in Durham that day to collect his force's wages. And two days before the murder Wright had gone to police headquarters asking where the superintendent would be during the next few days.

The jury returned a verdict that Benjamin Wright had murdered Superintendent Scott and had then committed suicide in a state of temporary insanity.

On the day following the murder five minutes' silence was observed in the courts in which the superintendent had been a prominent figure. A crowd of at least 20,000 lined the route of his funeral in Jarrow on June 3rd, as a procession half a mile long made its way to St. Paul's church where the superintendent had read the lesson only the previous Sunday. Six sergeants acted as pall-bearers.

Meanwhile Benjamin Wright was buried quietly at Herrington, about a hundred mourners singing a hymn outside his cottage and then following his widow and four children to a graveside service at the cemetery.

Even in death the killer had contrived to point an accusing finger from the grave ... or rather from his mantelpiece where his garbled parting note was found.

"The only good this will do," he wrote, "is to be hoped will stimulate superintendents to always speak the truth, and not to resort to scientific lies when giving evidence against brother officers."

The note went on to say that it would be better if chief constables did not repose so much confidence in the superintendents upon whom they greatly depended.

But that wasn't all. As Wright's family went through his wardrobe in order to wash, press and put away his clothes his mother-in-law found another note in one of his pockets.

"This day shall the Lord deliver thee into my hands!" the note proclaimed. "Thus sayeth the Lord, he that cometh to me, though his sins be as scarlet, I will make thee white as snow ... the Lord is my redeemer."

So it seemed that Benjamin Wright had been motivated by more than his grievance. Religious mania had also come into it...

crowd and wondered what had happened. Then he saw the Chief Constable, who had by now had the two bodies removed from the street. Superintendent Scott had been taken to the Red Lion Inn nearby, Wright to the Castle Hotel.

The surgeon went first to the Red Lion where Scott lay in the passage. Checking his pulse and finding none, Dr. Vann confirmed that the superintendent had died, adding that little could have been done for him as a bullet had passed through his lungs.

Going next to the Castle Hotel, the doctor found Wright lying unconscious in the stables, blood oozing from his mouth. His pulse was weak, he had a wound on the left side of his mouth and throat and his left temple was swelling rapidly. As far as the surgeon could ascertain, the bullet with which Wright had shot himself was still in his head, for there was no exit wound.

Dr. Vann gave him pain-killers in the hope that they would also help to keep his

heart beating, and did his best to stem the flow of blood from Wright's mouth. Fifteen minutes later, however, Benjamin Wright died without regaining consciousness.

Post-mortem examinations established the fact that Superintendent Scott had been

Wright's face was covered in blood and there was a crack in his skull

shot through his seventh rib. There was a scorch mark on the back of his coat from the muzzle of Wright's rifle, while there was a round hole in the superintendent's vest that corresponded with the bullet's exit wound in his chest.

Wright's face was covered with blood. There was a crack in the top of his skull, and he had in effect blown his brains out.

At Jarrow the police court's business had just finished for the day when a telegram arrived from Durham. It was

appreciation of the assistance he had tried to give their fallen colleague. They paid his fine for him, so instead of going to prison he was able to return home.

A Silver Street shopkeeper told the court that he was looking out of his window when he saw Superintendent Scott pass his shop with Fannen handcuffed to him, walking in the middle of the road. He then saw Wright who appeared to be following them, holding a rifle. Gaining on the two, Wright rammed the rifle into the superintendent's back and fired. It all happened so quickly, said the shopkeeper, that he was powerless to give any warning.

The Chief Constable said that a search had failed to find the bullet which had passed through the superintendent's body. He had found the rifle lying in the road beside Scott. A six-chambered German revolver lay nearby, in which only one bullet had been used.

The coroner told the jury that Wright had evidently nursed a feeling of resentment

The big wheel at Whitley Bay amusement park where the showground illusion Miller's Ghost would have been seen

On the afternoon of Friday, September 20th, 1901, two men walked along Huddlestone Street (right) in the seaside resort of Cullercoats. Heading for number 55, they had come on a mission ... The murder of Joseph Ferguson

THOUSANDS HAD flocked to see the showground illusion known as "Miller's Ghost." Over the years it had made a fortune for Mr. Miller, its proprietor. But at the turn of the century it was to lead to three men losing their lives ...

The money amassed from Miller's Ghost had been left to Miller's widow, who had subsequently remarried. Her 67-year-old second husband, Joseph Ferguson, was 18 years her junior and the same age as her eldest son John Miller, a showman and dealer who with his two brothers now found himself disinherited. The nest-egg gleaned from the exhibition of Miller's Ghost would go to Ferguson, whose 85-year-old wife was unlikely to live much longer.

This was the situation which led to events in 1901 which set all Tyneside talking. In the dock at

VENGEANCE MURDER IN CULLERCOATS BAY

Illusionist's fortune motive for killing

Northumberland Assizes in Newcastle stood John Miller, 67, accused of murdering his stepfather of the same age. On trial with him was his nephew, another John Miller, a 30-year-old musician.

The judge, Mr. Justice Grantham, had never known anything like it. Checking court records, he found that Newcastle had not had such a case of an uncle and nephew accused of murder for 117 years.

The bizarre events had begun ordinarily enough on the afternoon of Friday, September 20th, 1901, in an

Cullercoats Bay. The two men were seen leaning on the railings looking out to sea before crossing the road and going into the Bay Hotel

ironmonger's shop run by George Purvis in Saville Street, North Shields. The two Millers, uncle and nephew, had walked into the shop saying they wanted to see some knives. Purvis produced a display case containing 18 knives and placed it on the counter for their inspection.

"They aren't the kind of knife we want," said the elder Miller after examining them. Indicating to his nephew, he added: "He's going to sea as a cook."

"Then it's a sheath knife you want," said Purvis.

The elder Miller nodded, but when the ironmonger produced one it was rejected as too long. Purvis then opened a package containing a dozen knives an inch shorter than the first sheath knife he had offered.

"You are murdering my husband!" the old woman shouted at her son and nephew. Then Ferguson slumped down at the foot of the stairs

"This will do," said the uncle, selecting one.

They'd need a sheath and a belt to go with it, Purvis told them, putting a sheath on the counter and going to the other side of the shop to fetch a suitable belt.

Meanwhile the nephew had slipped the knife into the sheath. The ironmonger handed him the belt to try on. The younger Miller put it round his waist but then took it off, saying he only wanted the knife and sheath and never mind the belt.

Purvis thought this odd, but put it down to drink. The nephew seemed unsteady on his feet. He took his change, handed it to his uncle, and the two left the shop.

They then went to the sea front at Cullercoats, a seaside resort situated at the southern end of Whitley Bay. They arrived there at about 3.30 p.m. and caught the eye of several people. Zephaniah Miller, a cab driver who was not related to the pair but knew them, saw John Miller and his nephew leaning over the railings, looking out to sea and apparently whispering to each other.

Then he saw them cross the street, go into the Bay Hotel and come out again a few minutes later. The nephew disappeared up a nearby back lane momentarily and then rejoined his uncle, to whom he whispered something. The two then walked away up Huddlestone Street.

The Millers were also noticed by the errand boy at Robertson's the grocers. He watched in amusement as they went up the road, the nephew apparently staggering-drunk. On reaching 55 Huddlestone Street they stopped and the younger Miller

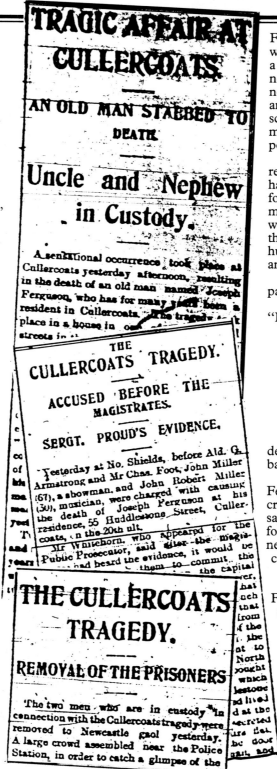

TRAGIC AFFAIR AT CULLERCOATS

AN OLD MAN STABBED TO DEATH

Uncle and Nephew in Custody.

A sensational occurrence took place at Cullercoats yesterday afternoon, resulting in the death of an old man named Joseph Ferguson, who has for many years been a resident in Cullercoats. The tragedy took place in a house in one of the streets in ...

THE CULLERCOATS TRAGEDY.

ACCUSED BEFORE THE MAGISTRATES.

SERGT. PROUD'S EVIDENCE.

Yesterday at No. Shields, before Ald. G. Armstrong and Mr Chas. Foot, John Miller (67), a showman, and John Robert Miller (30), musician, were charged with causing the death of Joseph Ferguson at his residence, 55 Huddlestone Street, Cullercoats, on the 20th ult.

Mr Whitehorn, who appeared for the Public Prosecutor, said after the magistrates had heard the evidence, it would be ... them to commit ... the capital ...

THE CULLERCOATS TRAGEDY.

REMOVAL OF THE PRISONERS

The two men who are in custody in connection with the Cullercoats tragedy were removed to Newcastle gaol yesterday. A large crowd assembled near the Police Station, in order to catch a glimpse of the ...

pounded the door with his fist, ignoring the large knocker.

The errand boy's curiosity was aroused when he saw the elder Miller step into an adjacent doorway as if to hide. Then the nephew pushed his way into number 55, saying "Hello, there!" to Joseph Ferguson who had opened the door. The elder Miller now emerged from the nearby doorway and followed his nephew inside.

The scene was also observed by the boy's employer, James Melville, watching through his shop window. His attention attracted by the nephew's hammering on the door, Melville watched the two enter number 55 and then saw old Mrs.

Ferguson open the front-room window upstairs. She called down to a passing boy to knock on a neighbour's door. When the neighbour came out she looked up and saw Mrs. Ferguson who was screaming that her husband had been murdered and asked her to fetch the police.

Joseph Ferguson had been stabbed repeatedly in the neck, chest and hands. Slumping to the floor at the foot of the stairs, he died within minutes. Mrs. Ferguson had witnessed the scene from the top of the stairs. "You are murdering my husband!" she shouted to her son and his nephew.

Rushing up the stairs, they pushed past her.

"There, old woman," said her son. "He's dead. We've stabbed him to

"... I will die a coward. Never, before God, had I any intention of doing it. I will go to the scaffold and die ..."

death." Then they went down the back stairs that led into the yard.

Neighbours attracted by Mrs. Ferguson's screams were now crowding the back lane where they saw the elder Miller search his pocket for a match to light his pipe. His nephew had blood on his hands and coat and complained that his head was hot.

Mrs. Isabella Mason, told by Mrs. Ferguson that her husband had been murdered, went into the house, saw his body on the floor and then stepped out into the back yard where she told the Millers, "Ferguson has been stabbed."

"Yes, four or five times," said the elder Miller, at which his nephew spun round and shouted: "You tantalised me, you irritated me, you gave me the drink and you gave me the knife!"

The uncle glared but said nothing.

Turning to Mrs. Mason, the nephew asked her to feel his head, saying it was hot. When she declined he bathed his forehead in a barrel of water in the back yard.

Police Constable Whitehead now arrived. Shouldering his way through the crowd, he arrested the Millers. The uncle looked at him blankly when cautioned. The nephew, his eyes rolling and froth coming from his mouth, appeared deranged.

Examining the body, Dr. John Phillips, the assistant police surgeon, found that Joseph Ferguson had received eight stab wounds, two of them fatal. The cause of death had been severance of the carotid artery, haemorrhage and a severed windpipe. "He had no chance at all,"

Saville Street, North Shields, where an uncle and his nephew bought the murder weapon in an ironmonger's shop

said the doctor.

After placing the Millers in cells Constable Whitehead returned to the murder scene and soon found the bloodstained knife lying by the body.

At about 5.45 p.m. Dr. Ernest Brumwell, the police surgeon, saw the Millers at North Shields police station. The uncle was quiet, but the nephew was becoming hysterical and had clearly been drinking.

On the final visit before his execution the youth clung so desperately to his mother that he had to be dragged away by warders

"I done it, I done it!" he told the doctor. "Take me and hang me! I have murdered him!"

Cautioned by Sergeant William Proud, who told him there would be plenty of time for him to say what he had to say later, the nephew replied: "That's all right. I'm going to die. I have done something to make me die. It's true that I've committed murder. I will die a coward. Never, before God, had I any intention of doing it. I will go to the scaffold and die ... I feel miserable to think that I have had no provocation to do it."

His uncle interjected: "I have nothing to do with the affair. I tried to prevent it but could not. I have as little to do with it as you have."

Dr. Brumwell found that the younger Miller had blood on his hands, face and clothes, and a wound on the palm of his right hand. The uncle had light bloodstains on the breast of his coat and on his left ear.

Charged with Ferguson's murder, the elder Miller said: "I know nothing about it. I am as innocent as a child unborn. I believe that if I had my eyesight I could have stopped it, at least to a great extent."

His nephew said: "I simply say I deserve what I get for being such a fool. I was mad with drink or I wouldn't have done such a thing. I'm very sorry."

But when he appeared at Northumberland Assizes on November 15th, 1901, and was asked what he pleaded, he said, "I can't say I am guilty." His uncle pleaded "Not guilty."

Mr. J. E. Joel, prosecuting, told the court that rows had broken out in the

Newcastle at the time of the double hanging in the city

Miller family after the former Mrs. Miller, now Mrs. Ferguson, made a will in which her second husband was the sole beneficiary. This had led to Joseph Ferguson's murder.

Mr. Horace Marshall, defending the younger Miller, said that his client admitted his role in the murder

The Esplanade, Whitley Bay. The tranquil seaside resort was shocked by the violent attack just along the coast at Cullercoats

but had been insane when it was committed.

James Miller told the court that his brother, the younger John Miller, had lain unconscious for three days after being kicked on the head by a horse when he was seven. This had changed his personality. Previously bright and cheerful, he had become sullen, would sit in a corner staring into space and had become known as "Silly Jack."

The one way to get him to do something was to tell him he daren't do it. Then, regardless of whether it was right or wrong, he would spring into action. When agitated he would fall down, kick out and bite skin from his arms, looking and acting like a maniac.

The defence presented medical evidence that the younger John Miller had spent four months in an asylum two years previously under treatment for mania induced by drink. But the medical superintendent of another asylum, appearing for the prosecution, said that he had examined the younger defendant in October and believed he had known what he was doing on the day of the murder. The medical officer at Newcastle's gaol, where the nephew was now confined, said that the nephew had been suffering from delirium tremens but had now recovered.

Calling Mrs. Mary Ferguson as a witness, Mr. Joel warned the judge and jury that because of her age she might find it difficult to understand the proceedings and to make herself understood.

As she entered the witness box the court usher noticed that she had something hidden under her coat. Asked what this was, she revealed a puppy which she continued to stroke. The sight of this caused a ripple of laughter around the court, and even Mr. Justice Grantham permitted himself a smile.

Mr. Joel asked her if any of the Millers had stayed with her or had visited her? After looking around the court her gaze settled ahead, but she said she was sorry her memory wasn't now all that good and she would have to think hard. "They may have stopped for a week or two a few years ago but they hadn't stopped, they may have visited, but that was all," she recalled.

"Then there couldn't have been any quarrelling or ill-feeling between them?" Mr. Joel asked. Shaking her head, she replied, "No, that is, unless there was anything in their mind about money."

"But you never heard any quarrels?" Mr. Joel repeated, this time forcefully.

"No, if they had kept themselves right they would have been all right."

She started to ramble, telling the court that she had always shown them kindness and had given them money, sometimes a lot.

Mr. Justice Grantham, who by now was starting to tire of her ramblings, interjected. "She never saw any quarrelling, or anything between the accused or her husband?" the judge asked Mr. Joel to confirm.

Mr. Joel asked her a few more questions, and then went through the events of the day on which the murder was committed. Mr. Justice Grantham, seemingly losing his patience, cut in, asking her, "Did you see anything in their hands?"

"No, sir, I did not, or I would be very glad to tell you," she answered. Referring to the knife that had killed her husband in a voice now steadily rising, the judge said to her, "Look at that, do you remember ever having seen anything like that?" Shaking her head she replied, "No, not to my memory I don't." She then went on to say that she knew the elder prisoner in the dock — it was, of course, her son — had lost the sight of one eye although she couldn't remember which one. There were sniggers throughout the court and Mr. Justice Grantham glared at Mr. Joel as the old lady left the witness box.

Mr. Marshall told the court that on the day of the murder his client had missed his train for Brampton, had been drinking heavily and had met his uncle by chance.

If, Mr. Marshall continued, the elder Miller harboured ill-feeing towards Ferguson and chose some agent to do him harm, what was more likely than that he should choose his nephew? The younger Miller had been in just the sort of mood in which delusions would be likely to occur.

For the elder John Miller, Mr. Mitchell Innes, defending, reminded the jury that it was the nephew who had confessed three or four times. "No one would contend that it was the hand of the elder Miller that struck the fatal blow."

Summing up, Mr. Justice Grantham told the jury that they had to consider why the elder Miller had gone into the doorway adjoining 55 Huddleston Street if not to hide. He had not attempted to save the victim but had stood by while the attack was carried out. He had said that Ferguson was stabbed four or five times so he must have seen what took place, yet he had cited his eyesight as an excuse.

In view of such evidence, the judge continued, could the jury say that a man in the elder Miller's position — sober, older, stronger than his nephew – was not responsible and had no part in the murder committed under his very eyes?

Referring to the younger Miller's confessions, the judge said that if he made himself drunk for the purpose of committing a crime, going to the Bay Hotel to get Dutch courage, he would be liable.

After retiring for only 10 minutes the jury returned to find both Millers guilty of wilful murder.

Sentencing them to death, Mr. Justice Grantham singled out the uncle for particular attention. "No one can doubt that you went with your nephew," he told him. "He was the younger man, with you and under your influence, and although he was responsible for his actions he was much worse for drink than you. You could have controlled him if you wanted ... It is impossible to come to any other conclusion than that you knew what was going to happen."

While the elder Miller seemed indifferent to his fate on the eve of the double execution, his nephew became hysterical, clinging to his mother on her final visit and having to be dragged away by warders.

In view of the nephew's hysteria it was decided that the two prisoners should not be placed on the scaffold together, the governor of Newcastle Gaol saying that it would be unwise to let them see each other. The elder Miller was consequently hanged at 8 a.m. on December 7th, 1901, his nephew following him to the gallows 90 minutes later.

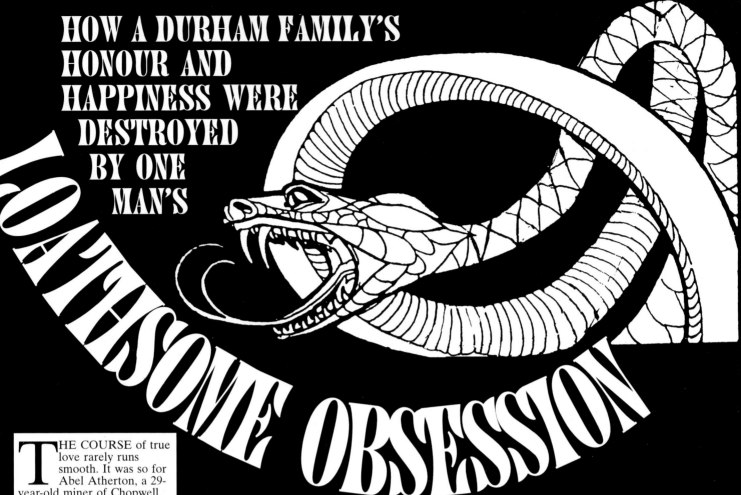

HOW A DURHAM FAMILY'S HONOUR AND HAPPINESS WERE DESTROYED BY ONE MAN'S LOATHSOME OBSESSION

THE COURSE of true love rarely runs smooth. It was so for Abel Atherton, a 29-year-old miner of Chopwell, County Durham. The love of his life never had any intention of returning his affection. But then, she was only 15.

Abel Atherton had worked for most of his adult life as a miner in various collieries around the North-East. Although a Lancastrian from Wigan, he had settled in Chopwell where he lodged with the Patricks at 20 Thames Lane.

His life revolved around going to work ... and admiring the Patricks' pretty 15-year-old daughter, Frances Mary. He watched her develop and often managed to kiss her and hold her round the waist. Frances thought it all innocent — after all, she did the same thing with her father.

But Atherton read more into it and began making improper suggestions, which scared her. Frustrated by this and her coldness, he started insinuating that her behaviour with her father was unnatural. This was a slur he was to repeat over and over again.

On Saturday, July 24th, 1909, Frances could stand the lodger and his insinuations no longer. When Jacob Patrick, her mild-mannered father, came home from work at around 1 p.m., Frances told him that if Atherton didn't go she would leave. Jacob had little choice. He wouldn't hear of his daughter leaving, and he ordered Atherton to go

straight away.

Making a show of gathering his things, the miner departed with his box, gramophone, and his beloved gun. He didn't go far, just a few streets away to Mrs. Isabella Forster's house in Mersey Street. Moving in, he complained bitterly of how he had been treated by the Patricks. He went on to tell a

As Atherton became more bold in his suggestions, Frances became more scared, and told her father

shocked Isabella that he hadn't done anything wrong. It was Frances and her father, he said, repeating his startling insinuations.

"It's a good job I left the Patricks before I did some mischief," he continued. "I have carried these about all day." He reached into his pocket, producing three cartridges. "One of these was meant for Frances, one for Patrick, and one for myself."

Mrs. Forster told him to put them away as she didn't want anything like that in her house. Atherton nodded, saying he would lock them safely away

in his box.

As he passed his old lodgings the next day he paused for a word with the Patricks' next-door neighbour who was sitting on the step. "I'll finish the lot next door," Atherton threatened. The neighbour said nothing, but when Atherton had gone he went next door and told Frances what had been said.

Frances nodded, thinking nothing of it. She was used to Atherton's threats.

He continued to visit the Patricks although he wasn't made welcome. He was at the house again on the night of August 8th when he staggered in uninvited and the worse for drink. Turning to Frances, he said it had been through her that he had been forced to leave. "You have done your worst for me," he told her, "and I will do my worst for you, as I can see I'm not wanted here."

He was back the next day and the day after that, each time appearing more threatening than the last.

On the night of August 10th, on seeing Mrs. Elizabeth Patrick sitting in the kitchen he asked, "How are you getting on?"

"We're all right," she replied.

Atherton was now smiling.

Turning to Frances, he asked her if she still kissed her father.

"There's no reason why I should stop it," she replied. "He is my father and nobody has anything to do with it. There is nothing wrong."

Still smiling, Atherton disagreed. "If I took it to court," he told her, "you would get wrong for it."

"I don't see how we could get wrong," Frances retorted. "I have done it many times in the presence of my mother."

At 10 a.m. on Wednesday, August 11th, he again walked into the house uninvited.

"I have brought you this letter which I said I would write to you," he told Frances, handing it to her. She opened it, noticing that it was addressed to her mother, and started to read it. Half-way through it she crumpled it up and threw it on the fire.

"What do you think about yourself?" she asked him. "If you have not a heart, my mother and father have."

He looked at her steadily before replying, "If you have a heart I will break yours." Then

TRAGEDY AT CHOPWELL.

Young Married Woman Fatally Shot.

Miner Arrested and Charged with Murder.

On Wednesday night a tragedy occurred at Chopwell, the victim being a married woman, named Elizabeth Ann Patrick, aged 31 years, the wife of Jacob Patrick, a miner, living in Thames Street, Chopwell. In connection with the affair Abel Atherton, a miner, 29 years of age, was taken into custody.

It appears that Atherton, who is a native of Wigan, in Lancashire, had worked for some time as a miner at Chopwell, and had lodged with the Patricks. About three weeks ago he left his lodgings, and, prior to that it is alleged that he had paid some attention to the daughter, Frances Mary Patrick, who is only 15 years of age. These attentions were, it appears, resented by the parents, and Atherton went to live at another home in the village.

He walked out, accusing her again of unnatural behaviour.

Frances had a lot to do that day. Giving Atherton plenty of time to make his way back to his lodgings, to the pit or wherever he was going, she grabbed her coat and shopping basket and left the house.

When she returned home at about a quarter to six that night she found Atherton there again, sitting talking to her mother. On seeing Frances come into the room he started to complain to her mother about the way she behaved with her father. But Elizabeth Patrick stopped him in midstream, saying she was sick of the mischief he was causing, and she would have it all proved. Standing up, she told him to clear out and not to come back. "Yes," she told him, "if it's not true what you have been saying, there will be trouble for you."

"It will be trouble for someone else," Atherton replied, shaking his head.

Then he went back to his lodgings where Mrs. Forster saw him checking his gun. When she asked what he was doing he said he was going to have a bit of sport. There were tears in his eyes as he said goodbye to her and her son, thanking her for all she had done for him and for taking him in.

As he tucked the rifle under his arm Mrs. Forster begged him not to take it out.

"Stand back or I'll shoot," he warned her, leaving by the back door.

Mrs. Forster hurried to her front door and waited on the step, anxiously. She had no idea of what she could expect to happen, but she had a foreboding that it would be terrible. Atherton's mood was black, and she knew he wasn't fooling when he took the gun with him.

Half an hour or less after leaving the Forster house he barged into the Patricks' kitchen. There the whole family were sitting with their neighbour, Elizabeth Marlowe, pleasantly chatting about the day's events over a

Mrs. Patrick made a lunge for the gun-barrel and pointed it away from the people in the room

large pot of tea and a plate of biscuits.

Seeing the gun, Mrs. Patrick was on her feet in a trice. "What are you going to do with that?" she cried. "You are not going to use that here!"

There was a deathly silence. Mrs. Marlowe was too dumbfounded by the obvious menace to say anything. Jacob Patrick, wedged between wall and table, remained mute and still, fearing that any movement on his part would galvanise the ex-tenant to some terrible action. As for Frances, she cowered in her chair, so scared that her heartbeats were almost audible.

Only Elizabeth Patrick had the presence of mind to break the spell and put this impasse to an end. As Atherton stood there, unmoved, she made a frantic clutch at the barrel of the gun, pointing it away from the shocked assembly.

Frances moved to help her mother, but Mrs. Marlowe held her back as Atherton and Elizabeth Patrick began to struggle. A shot rang out, the bullet going wide and ending up in the street. Then the gun went off again.

Mary Cruddas, a fifteen-year-old neighbour, was passing the Patricks' back door when she heard the report. She stood transfixed as Elizabeth Patrick staggered out crying, "Oh; my leg!" before collapsing in a heap. Then Mary saw a rifle sail through the air to land just past Mrs. Patrick.

Isabella Forster, still standing at her front door, also heard the two shots. Wincing, she stood for a minute or so before going back into her house. She knew that she had seen the last of her lodger.

Atherton was meanwhile making a pathetic attempt to cut his throat with the pen-knife he always carried. Then he stepped over Elizabeth's body, taking care to avoid the pool of blood. He bent, kissed her, and then walked away.

Hearing the shooting, a neighbour had run to find a policeman. Constable John Coulson was on his way, walking down Thames Street when Atherton went up to him and said, "I am the man you want. She is quite dead. It is a pity I did not finish myself off as well, it's a bad job for me."

Right there in the street Coulson frisked him and found 12 ball cartridges, a pocket-knife, and a letter written by Atherton dated July 18th, 1909. The note read:

"Dear Chum,

I received your letter and am very sorry to hear you have lost your money. But I do believe you are born unlucky. I have been very lucky until this month or two. You will very likely know what I have told you, and what you said when you were at our house yourself about the daughter and father carrying on. It is all through the carry on that I have done what I have done.

"I have tried my hand the same road, and I have been unlucky as well as you, for I tried it on, but it did not come off as I expected. But never mind, cheer up, we have been the best of friends. You are the only friend I have in the world

— when you get this letter I will be in a different world. I told her if we got catched I would do the job for her and myself as well and she's turned her back on me.

"They will think I am daft. But I am tired of living, I have my senses Dick, and she is thick with her father, as anybody what is married is with their wives. I have written this for fear I do not get catched and as soon as I get catched it must be the finish for both of us. So this is the last letter from your old chum,

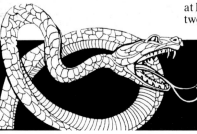

Atherton's letter to his brother showed that he believed his own lies about the incest between Frances and her father. And so many locals finally believed it that Frances had to undergo a medical examination and get a

Abel Atherton — Goodbye for ever. These letters is what Frances Mary wrote to me, she needed to tice me always. She had wrote many dozens letters, and I have burned them. She

The inspector was silent as Atherton rambled on about how he had not fired the gun at Mrs. Patrick

has a key to fit my box, she used to leave them in the box."

PC Coulson took Atherton back to the Patricks' house, where a large crowd had gathered around Elizabeth's body. Frances was cradling her mother's head, crying.

Coulson could find no pulse — Jacob Patrick said he had already done so. Now all he could do was stand around, impotent and useless with shock. The policeman found the rifle where it had landed, and checked the chamber. It had been fired twice, which tallied with the two discharged cartridges that had been found. Apart from making the firearm safe there was little

more he could do at the scene, so he marched Atherton to Blaydon police station.

On being charged with attempting to commit suicide, and with Elizabeth Patrick's murder, he replied: "The knife was not sharp enough. The other was a pure accident. She fired one shot in the air, and the other she shot herself."

The clothes Elizabeth Patrick was wearing at the time of her death had already been examined. Two gun-wads had been found close together, adhered with fresh blood to the inside of her chemise.

The next day Atherton was taken to Gateshead police station, escorted by Sergeant Loston and Inspector Dryden. In the cab the prisoner turned to the inspector and asked, "Is she dead?"

Inspector Dryden said this was so. "There's one thing that consoles me," Atherton told him, "I did not shoot her. She shot herself." The inspector said nothing as Atherton continued: "Little Joe in the office told me about a man who wanted a gun, and I was going to try and sell it to him. On the way I called at the house to frighten them. She

Gateshead High Street (above) where Abel Atherton was photographed being escorted to the police station

certificate of virginity before the ugly rumours that had destroyed the honour of her family could be quashed. At last Atherton's jealousy of the normal displays of affection were revealed for what they were, and his own improper intentions towards young Frances were finally believed by everyone

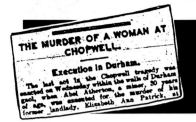

THE MURDER OF A WOMAN AT CHOPWELL

Execution in Durham.

The last act in the Chopwell tragedy was enacted on Wednesday within the walls of Durham gaol, when Abel Atherton, a miner, 30 years of age, was executed for the murder of his former landlady, Elizabeth Ann Patrick, at

During the years Atherton had lodged with the Patrick family, he had become increasingly more obsessed with the 15-year-old daughter, whom he had known

THE EXECUTION OF ABEL ATHERTON...

As recalled by the hangman and a local newspaper reporter.

Henry Pierrepoint recalled:
"It was a cold wintry day when I arrived at Durham on the afternoon before the execution. I called in at a hotel opposite the prison from where the landlord used to send our meals across to the prison. While I was talking to the landlord at the counter, who should come in but Atherton's father and sister-in-law in deep mourning dress. Atherton's father was talking about his son and saying he was innocent. He pulled out some last letters they had just received from him while paying their last visit. I took a seat until they had gone, and pretended to interest myself in some curios that hung on the wall. It was now time for us to go to the prison, and as I was walking across the road I saw Atherton's father and sister-in-law standing watching to see if I went into the prison. I knew they had guessed from my speech who I was when they came into the hotel.

"I made my usual arrangements after my arrival. Then I went to Atherton's cell. I found him fairly cheerful, but a sad, downcast look upon him. He was only of short stature, 5 feet 1¼ inches high, but of strong build."

A local newspaper reporter wrote: "After the visit from his father Atherton seemed reconciled, and retired to rest at about 10 o'clock on Tuesday night. He slept pretty well, and at half-past five was aroused, washed, and dressed in his own clothing. The chaplain arrived at the gaol before 7 o'clock, and administered the communion to Atherton in the condemned cell. Atherton partook of a light breakfast, after which the chaplain again joined him, and remained with the condemned man until a few minutes to eight, then he left to robe to take part in the final act. Wednesday morning broke clear and frosty. At ten minutes to eight Mr. A. W. Wilson, acting under-sheriff, entered the prison, and was followed by the three press representatives. Dr. Gilbert was the last of the officials to enter. Principal Warder Hunt took charge of the press men, and at about four minutes to eight conducted them to a position immediately in front of the execution shed. Warders were already in position, at a signal from Engineer Stanton, to throw back the doors of the execution shed, and officers were stationed to signal to Warder Elliott, who has ascended to the prison bell, ready to toll the passing knell. Although all was perfectly quiet within the walls, imagination readily supplied the grim details which were being enacted within the prison."

Pierrepoint later recalled:
"When all the officers arrived to witness the last dread act, I entered the condemned cell. Atherton was looking a little terrified. I pinioned his arms and prepared his neck. Then I gently tapped him on the shoulder, and said, 'Keep your pluck up, my lad.' This put life in him. I said I would get it over as quickly as possible. I brought him into the corridor. The procession started."

The reporter, who was obviously one of the witnesses at the hanging, then went on:
"The colliery buzzers had commenced to sound, and the first stroke of eight on the clock over the assize courts had sounded, when the voice of the chaplain was heard reciting the opening sentence of the burial service. A second later the procession came in view.

"The culprit, who seemed remarkably calm and composed, and walked with a firm step, fixed the press representative with a look which betokened that he had something to communicate. However, the procession hurried on, and Atherton saw the preparations which had been made for the carrying out of the dread sentence. From the beam there was the rope reaching well nigh to the floor. On the drop there was the ankle strap lying ready for use, and across the drop there were two stout boards with foot-pieces, ready for the attendant warders to render Atherton assistance if required.

"At the door the chaplain stepped aside, and the remainder of the procession passed inside. The moment the threshold had been passed,. Atherton's cap had been removed from his head, and the executioners urged him forward to the mark on the drop. The assistant instantly dropped on to his knees and fastened the ankle strap, and while Pierrepoint was adjusting the noose, Atherton in a husky voice cried out, 'Yer hanging an innocent man.' "

Pierrepoint later stated:
"Whether or not I could not flinch…I pulled the lever which gave Atherton a drop of 7 feet 3 inches, and launched him into the hereafter."

"Atherton shot from view," *the reporter carried on,* "before – incredible as it may seem – the clock had ceased striking…As the press representatives stepped forward and looked into the pit the body was hanging perfectly still. The execution house was then closed till 9 o'clock, when the executioners withdrew the body from the pit, released it from the rope and removed the other paraphernalia of their dread office."

took the gun from me and shot herself. She went to the door and the gun went off, she shot herself with the second shot. I would have stopped her but the daughter held me, and Mrs. Marlowe stood in front of me and stopped me."

Abel Atherton appeared briefly at Gateshead Magistrates' Court later that day, when evidence of his arrest was given by PC Coulson.

The constable said that when Atherton was first charged with Elizabeth Patrick's murder he replied: "I think she shot herself, but I have been the instigator of it — I wish I had finished myself at the same time."

When Inspector Dryden applied for him to be remanded in custody, Atherton protested: "I never shot the woman. I went to the house …"

He was interrupted by the chairman of the bench who advised him to reserve his statement for later.

"I am not guilty of shooting the woman!" Atherton shouted as he was led away, remanded in custody to

For two years Atherton had lived under the Patricks' roof, and thought well of the family

Durham Prison.

At Elizabeth Patrick's inquest on August 17th, her daughter Frances said that Atherton had repeatedly made improper and immoral suggestions to her, which she had rebuffed. She could remember her mother lying shot on the footpath outside the back door and Atherton standing in the middle of the kitchen. After that she could recall little more. She had tried to help her mother, she said tearfully, but Mrs. Marlowe had restrained her.

Jacob Patrick, conscious of gossip arising from Atherton's allegations against him, had asked Dr. Bulkley of Chopwell to examine Frances. Dr. Bulkley had consequently examined the girl at his surgery, and in a note to the coroner he had written: "I can

give positive evidence as to the existence of her virginity. Mr. Patrick is very anxious that I should give evidence to this effect at the inquest, so as to silence the foul gossip which he says is prevalent in the village."

After 15 minutes' retirement the jury returned a verdict of 'wilful murder' against Abel Atherton. Mr. Graham, the coroner, then told the court: "I think I may take it upon myself to say that the jury are satisfied that the allegations made against Patrick and his daughter are wholly unfounded."

When Atherton appeared again before Gateshead magistrates on August 27th, Mr. Prynne, prosecuting, said that Mrs. Patrick had been shot in the thigh. She had died almost immediately through shock, the severing of her main arteries and a massive haemorrhage. Mr. Prynne said that Atherton's claim that he had taken his gun to the Patricks' house merely to frighten them was "utter poppycock."

Mr. Edward Clark, defending, asked Frances whether her mother had, as had been suggested, grabbed hold of the barrel of the gun. Frances replied that she couldn't remember as Mrs. Marlowe was holding her back.

Mr. Clark, asking Frances to be careful, reminded her of her evidence at the inquest. She had been quite sure then, he pointed out, that her mother had grabbed hold of the barrel.

Turning to Atherton's allegations, Mr. Clark said: "I don't make any suggestions, but when Atherton made the statements you have spoken about, did he appear very cross?"

"He was not well suited," Frances replied.

"Well, you put it that way, but was he vexed about it?"

"Yes, sir."

"So it seemed whether it was true or not, to have an effect on him?"

"Yes, sir," Frances replied.

Jacob Patrick, tall and gaunt, told the court that as soon as he had been made aware of what Atherton was getting up to, as his tenant, he had told him to leave immediately, which he did. He said that Atherton had never accused him to his face of any misconduct with his daughter.

"If he had accused you," asked Mr. Clark, "or you had heard such a thing, you would have thought it an imagination on his part, and a foolish one?"

"Yes, I would," said Mr. Patrick.

Fourteen-year-old Joseph, the Patricks' son, swore that Atherton was holding the gun when both shots were fired. He said he could remember his mother having hold of the gun also when the first shot was fired.

Committed for trial, Atherton again shouted as he was led from the court. "She shot herself!" he cried before being bundled hurriedly down the steps.

He pleaded not guilty to the murder charge when his trial before Mr. Justice Walton began at Durham Assizes on November 10th, 1909.

Mr. Griffith Jones had been retained for the defence. Seeking a manslaughter verdict, he was later to suggest to the court that Atherton's gun had gone off accidentally.

For the Crown, Mr. Lowenthal told the jury: "The suggestion of the prosecution is that Atherton deliberately fired the gun."

Atherton told the court that he had lived with the Patricks for more than two years, always getting on well with Elizabeth as well as the rest of

He admitted that he had fallen in love with her, despite her tender years

the family. He said Elizabeth "was more like a mother to me." He had thought a lot of her, and he was sure that she thought a lot of him. He claimed he also got along quite well with Frances, until he was thrown out. He admitted that he had fallen in love with her, despite her tender years, and that he had become jealous. He denied that he had intended from the outset to shoot Elizabeth Patrick. It had been his intention to sell the gun, he said, as he was hard up.

"If that were the case," asked Mr. Lowenthal, "why had he asked around to try and borrow a revolver?"

Atherton replied that he couldn't explain. He said he had never threatened Mrs. Patrick, but he admitted writing her a letter outlining what he claimed was going on between her husband and daughter.

He said he was "middling drunk" on the day of the shooting, but he could remember clearly what had happened. "Mrs. Patrick," he told the jury, "was a big woman." When he walked into the house she had jumped up, grabbed the gun with her left hand and pushed the barrel up, thrusting him away at the same time with her right hand.

Asked to explain how the gun had gone off, he said he couldn't. But he insisted that he hadn't shot anyone. He had never pulled the trigger. "Mrs. Patrick had the gun," he said, claiming that she had wrested it away from him.

Atherton sat back in the dock, his face cupped in both hands as he listened intently to Mr. Justice Walton summing up. Reminding the jury that the case for the defence was that the gun had gone off accidentally, he said that if they had any reasonable doubt it was their duty to acquit Atherton. "But," he continued, "if he fired the gun in such a way at Mrs. Patrick that any man in his senses would know it might kill her, it was wilful murder."

In conclusion, the judge outlined another possible scenario. What if Atherton had gone into the house with the gun, not intending to shoot anyone but perhaps intending to terrorise and intimidate them? And Mrs. Patrick, alarmed, rushed at him, got hold of the gun and in the ensuing struggle it went off owing to Atherton's carelessness and killed Mrs. Patrick? That might be manslaughter, said Mr. Justice Walton.

The jury filed out from the courtroom at two minutes to four, returning in just over half an hour, finding Abel Atherton guilty of murder.

Donning the black cap, the judge asked if he wished to say anything before the sentence was passed.

"Can I have a fresh trial?" Atherton asked with a slight smile.

Having faced up to his own jealousy regarding Frances, Atherton was ready to go to his death

In the condemned cell he continued to protest his innocence. Refused leave to appeal, he was destined to be the 84th person to be executed within Durham Prison since public executions were abolished.

"I write these few lines to you, hoping to find you all well," he wrote to his parents.

"You will very likely know the sad news before you get this letter — that there is no more hope for me in this world. I will have to put my trust in the Lord, he is the one who we all have to face sooner or later. There is one thing I will not have to answer for, and that is what I am sentenced to death for, of which I am innocent ...

"You can believe me what I told you is God's truth! It won't do me any good to tell lies. I would not have said anything if I had hold of the gun when she was shot, but I never was in the struggle. You will very likely get my box, and you can give Dick Symons them cartridges ... they'll be no good to anyone who has no gun ...

"I will expect you and Katie, Lizzie, and Levi coming on Monday if you can possibly get here. That is all at present, from your innocent son.

Abel Atherton."

On December 8th, 1909, snow started to fall heavily as he woke after a peaceful night. He made quick work of his breakfast and passed the next hour chatting with his two warders until the priest arrived.

He walked quickly and calmly to his place on the scaffold already marked by Henry Pierrepoint, who was assisted by William Willis. As Pierrepoint adjusted the noose, Atherton exclaimed, "You are hanging an innocent man." The lever was pulled and he dropped out of sight.

Outside snow continued to fall and no one viewed the notice which was pinned to the prison gate. Perhaps few cared any more. Abel Atherton certainly didn't.

BUTTERKNOWLE'S SHOCKING CRIME

COUNTLESS PEOPLE have passed a roadside plaque in the County Durham village of Butterknowle during the past century without giving it so much as a cursory glance. But that plaque was placed there for a reason long forgotten by all but the locals. It is the villagers' tribute to a policeman ...

There was driving rain and it was freezing on the night of Saturday, February 23rd, 1884. William Smith, newly promoted to his rank of police sergeant, shivered as he buttoned up his long overcoat whilst chatting with his wife at the front door of his cottage in Lynesack, a hamlet about three-quarters of a mile from Butterknowle, near Bishop Auckland.

The rain intensified as he was about to start on his beat to ensure that the local pubs closed on time. Glancing at his pocket watch, he saw that it was 9.20, so the pubs had another 40 minutes before they would have to close for the night. Waving goodbye to his wife Margaret, the sergeant set out on his short walk.

Half an hour later he was chatting to some men outside Butterknowle's Diamond Inn, known locally as the "Black Diamond". Three more men emerged from the warmth of the pub: Joseph Lowson and William Siddle, both 25, and Joseph Hodgson, 20.

Siddle promptly began shouting abuse at the sergeant — his custom whenever he saw him, for there had long been bad blood between them. At the annual Woodlands Gala the previous August, Smith had warned Siddle about his conduct. Siddle had responded by attacking the policeman, and the assault had cost him a hefty fine.

For Smith it had been just part of his day's work, but for Siddle the memory had rankled. He had since frequently declared just what he would like to do to all policemen: "Fight them and thrash them." He had repeated this threat at the New Year's supper at the Stag's Head in Butterknowle, leaving his companions in no doubt of what he would do to Smith or any other policeman who got in his way.

Now, outside the Diamond Inn, the three watched the sergeant continue on his beat. Shortly afterwards they split up. Hodgson and Lowson said they had a message to deliver, leaving Siddle as he walked along the road with several other men.

Suddenly Siddle stopped and said: "Let's rib [fight] the police!"

His companions ignored him. It was no weather to be fighting in, and they just wanted to get home out of it as quickly as possible.

Further along the road Siddle stopped again. "You are no company for me," he snarled at his companions, leaving them to see if he could find Lowson and Hodgson. Eventually he spotted them by the gate that led to the old engine house that was part of the disused Diamond Colliery.

Billy Parkin, on his way home, glanced at the new pocket watch his mother had bought for his birthday. He saw that the time was ten-past ten. He had just put his watch back in his pocket when he was grabbed by three men. Frightened and unsure of how to react, he stood quietly as he was jostled. Then he was allowed to go on his way, leaving the three men laughing behind him.

William Aikman, a tailor for more than 20 years, lived at Abbot's Houses on Butterknowle Lane. Looking out of his window, he saw it was raining heavily, but he had to deliver a suit he'd just finished.

On his short walk, as he

The arrow (far right), set in a wall, marks the spot where the policeman fell on the country road (above) after being stoned by drunken louts

POLICEMAN IN STREET

A gala at Woodland sparked bad feeling between Siddle and the sergeant who was savagely slain

STONED TO DEATH

Butterknowle surgeon, and his assistant Dr. Alfred Gorrick had spent the day in Bishop Auckland. On their way home they called at the Stag's Head, leaving a few minutes before 10 p.m. to head for their own fireside.

They were walking up the hill known as The Slack when a man passed them, muttering "Poor police!" over and over again.

Dr. Gorrick stopped the man and asked him what was the matter.

"He's killed!" the man cried.

"Who? Where?"

"Up there," the man replied, pointing.

Running along the road, Gorrick rounded a bend to see Sergeant Smith lying half on the pavement, half in the gutter. Bricks and stones were strewn on the road nearby. The doctor lifted the policeman's head (which was barely recognisable), and Smith groaned. His breathing was laboured, coming in short gasps.

Gorrick went back to fetch his colleague, who had been trailing behind him.

Examining the sergeant, Dr. Middleton raised his head and a piece of the skull fell away in his hand. One of the policeman's eyes hung from its socket, and some of his teeth were scattered on the ground. Opening Smith's mouth, Middleton found more broken teeth, which he removed.

The sergeant was clearly beyond medical help. All the doctors could do was to make his last minutes as comfortable as possible. Both were puzzled by the numerous lacerations on the policeman's hands.

Leaving Gorrick to do what he could, Middleton went to raise the alarm. He'd gone no more than 50 yards when he felt a violent blow on his chest. Looking to his right, he saw a barrage of bricks flying towards him, and he ran out of the line of fire.

Gorrick, hearing a noise, looked up to see three men approaching him. At the same time he saw Middleton at the top of the hill, shouting "Murder!"

At this the three men turned and walked quickly away. Gorrick followed them,

passed the old engine house he saw three men ahead of him, one tall, one of medium height and one shorter. As the tailor drew level with them the tallest of the trio bumped into him and he thought they were drunk. They were whispering together and laughing.

A hundred yards further on he met Sergeant Smith, who bade him a cheery "Goodnight" despite the foul weather.

Dr. John Middleton, a

but lost them near the old engine house. Looking up the road, he saw lanterns coming towards him as the road filled up with curious villagers. The doctor tried to enlist their help in catching the three men, but nobody seemed keen to pursue them.

Returning to where the sergeant lay, Gorrick together with Middleton and some of the villagers carried the policeman back to the cottage he had left just over an hour earlier. And there William Smith died an hour later without regaining consciousness.

Constable George Knight, informed of the sergeant's death, hurried to Lynesack and sent another constable to Staindrop, about six miles away, to fetch assistance.

Going to the scene of the attack with Dr. Middleton, Knight found several bricks with blood on them, together with a large piece of bloodstained sandstone. The search for evidence was continued by Sergeant James Daley on his arrival from Staindrop about two hours later.

Daley found a pearl button on the ground at the scene, and the names of Hodgson, Lowson and Siddle kept cropping up as he made more inquiries. Aware of Siddle's threats against Sergeant Smith, Daley and two constables headed for Siddle's home at Lands, a colliery hamlet about a mile from Butterknowle. They arrived to find Siddle and Hodgson in bed together at the cottage

belonging to Siddle's father.

Arresting them on suspicion of murder, Daley asked Hodgson to account for his movements during the night.

"I was at Simpson's [The Diamond Inn]," he replied.

"What time did you leave?"

"Ten o'clock."

"Who left with you?"

"Joe Lowson."

"On what road did you come home?"

Hodgson's jacket and trousers had been washed — and he didn't have another suit, he said at the time of his arrest

"Down Diamond Hill and across Bowes Hill."

"Had you a quarrel with anyone?"

"No."

"Did you see anyone leaving the public house until you arrived home?"

"No — I never saw anyone until Siddle overtook Lowson and me on Bowes Hill."

Answering the same questions, Siddle said he had left the pub with a lot of men. Ralph Blackett and another man had accompanied him as far as the old mill, and he had then proceeded alone to Bowes Hill, where he overtook Lowson and Hodgson. "We all three came home together. I was not drunk. I knew what I was doing."

Daley asked them for the

Lynesack, the neighbouring village where Sergeant Smith, father of seven, lived with his wife and family

clothes they had been wearing. He noticed that Hodgson's trousers seemed to have been recently washed. Hodgson asked for them back, saying he didn't have another pair. The sergeant returned them, but kept the suspects' boots and jackets.

He went next to Joseph Lowson's home about 150 yards away. Asked the same questions and giving similar answers, Lowson said only, "Is he dead?" on being told he was being arrested.

His jacket and trousers were

found drying in front of the fire. They had been washed — the jacket from the elbows downwards, and the trousers from the knees down.

Sergeant Daley's sister-in-law, Annie Hopper, often minded the police station in his absence. She was walking down the passage the next day to fetch some water when she heard Lowson call out to Siddle, who was in a separate cell.

"They cannot prove nowt against us," Lowson said. "They only have us on

How police looked in Sergeant Smith's day — little changed from the way they do today. Note the medals worn by some

Diamond Inn — then known
he Black Diamond

suspicion. Dinna tell them owt, Bill. Just say thou went straight home from Bowes Hill — thou knows it's reet, lad."

"Aye," Siddle replied.

On the following day Lowson's shirt was taken from him, Daley pointing out that one of its buttons was missing.

Lowson said nothing, but when he was back in his cell Siddle called to him: "Has thou been out, Joe?"

"Aye — the sergeant has had me out. Man, there's a button off my shirt neck — it was pulled off up yonder."

"Have they got the button?"

"I don't know. I expect so — they've kept my shirt and given me an old one."

On the same day Joseph Hodgson was taken before Barnard Castle magistrates. More than six feet tall, he towered over the policeman at his side and munched a sandwich he'd been given a few moments earlier. He appeared indifferent to the

proceedings, said nothing and was remanded in custody.

Meanwhile it was rumoured in Butterknowle that Siddle and Lowson had named Hodgson as the killer. They too appeared in court that day, singing loudly in their cells before they were brought before Staindrop magistrates and smiling broadly when they were told they were being remanded in custody.

When the inquest was opened at Royal Oak Inn at Butterknowle the next day Superintendent Thompson, from Barnard Castle, said that Sergeant Smith had been an exemplary officer, with more than 16 years' service. The sergeant was also the father of seven children.

Life came virtually to a standstill in Butterknowle and the surrounding villages two days later when the murdered officer was buried. Five policemen and the victim's 71-year-old father were the pall-bearers at the funeral, which was attended by hundreds, many weeping silently.

When the inquest was resumed at the Royal Oak the

The coroner reminded the jury that blood had been found on Lowson's clothes — but he thought murder had not been the intent

court heard that the button which Sergeant Daley had found matched those remaining on Lowson's shirt. Furthermore, the threads also matched.

Mr. W. Stock, a county analyst from Darlington, said he had found numerous bloodstains on Lowson's jacket and shirt, but he was unable to say if the blood were human.

Dr. Gorrick told the court that the man who had first alerted him and Dr. Middleton to the murder had promptly disappeared, but he believed he was the shorter of two men he had picked out at an identity parade held at Staindrop. Earlier, at a line-up of eight men at Barnard Castle police station, the doctor had identified the tallest man as one of the trio he had seen on the night of the murder.

Dr. Middleton testified that he had found Sergeant Smith lying on his left side with his legs drawn up. His cheekbone had been smashed in and most of his teeth had been knocked out.

Summing up, the coroner told the jury that a long chain of circumstantial evidence

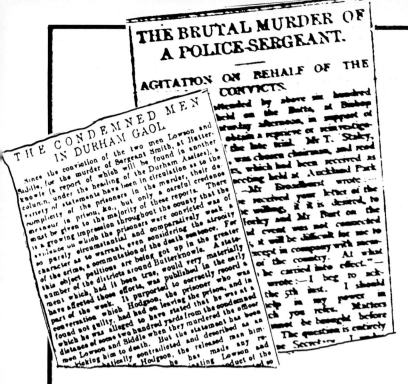

THE BRUTAL MURDER OF A POLICE-SERGEANT.

AGITATION ON BEHALF OF THE CONVICTS

THE CONDEMNED MEN IN DURHAM GAOL

Since the conviction of the two men Lowson and Siddle, for the murder of Sergeant Smith, at Butterknowle (a report of which will be found in another column, under the heading of the Durham Assizes), a variety of statements have been in circulation as to the complicity of the prisoners in the murder, their degree of more or less guilt, but only a careful credence must be given to the majority of these reports. There is a growing impression throughout the county that the evidence on which the prisoners were convicted was of so purely circumstantial and comparatively weak a character as to warrant, even considering the atrocity of the crime, a commutation of the death sentence. For this object petitions are being got up in the greater number of the districts around Butterknowle. A statement which, had it been true, would very materially have affected those efforts, was published in the early part of the week. It purported to correctly record a conversation which Hodgson, the prisoner who was found not guilty, had had on leaving the prison, and in which he was alleged to have stated that he was at a distance of some two hundred yards from the officer when Lowson and Siddle murdered the condemned men Lowson and Siddle to death. But the statement has been emphatically contradicted and described as an ... making him ... Hodgson, the released man say ... he ... eating ... duct ...

... attended by above one hundred ... held on the Barts, at Bishop ... Saturday afternoon, in support of ... obtain a reprieve or reim ... of the late trial ... Mr T. Staley, ... was chosen chairman, and read ... which had been received as ... meeting held at Auckland Park ... Mr Broadhurst wrote ... he received your letter of the ... stating, if it is desired, to ... Morley and Mr Burt on the ... and great care was not connected ... it will be difficult for me to ... accept in company with mem ... of the country. At what ... be carried into effect." — ... wrote:—I beg to ack ... the 5th inst. I should ... help in my power in ... which you refer. Matters ... must be brought before ... The question is entirely ... the Secretary ...

linked the three suspects to the murder — "They had all been at the Diamond Inn. They would have passed the spot where the murder was committed on their way home ..."

The coroner went on to remind the jury that blood had been found on Lowson's clothes, and when Lowson was arrested PC Knight had noticed blood on his cheek. Asked to account for this,

Lowson had replied: "I had a quarrel on the road home last night with Bill [Siddle]."

In conclusion, the coroner said that he thought the sergeant's killers hadn't intended to murder him, but the case was nevertheless one of murder and not manslaughter.

After an hour's deliberation the jury returned with a unanimous verdict of wilful murder against the three suspects.

At a further magistrates' hearing a week later, Dr. Middleton testified that in conducting a post-mortem examination he had found that

"I suppose there's two men sworn that I have been threatening Smith?" said Siddle to Constable Bonsfield at Staindrop police station

Sergeant Smith had died as a result of shock and massive blood loss, coupled with severe internal injuries inflicted by blows, kicks or bricks.

The doctor said he had found sand or some form of grit between the scalp and the skull, which had been shattered into seven pieces, parts of it falling away at his touch. The sergeant's truncheon was still in his pocket, indicating that he hadn't had time to draw it. Lacerations to his hands had been caused by his holding his head to protect it, or in scraping his hands along the ground in an effort to evade the blows or bricks.

Dr. Middleton went on to say that when he later identified the three men who had thrown bricks at him on

the night of the murder Siddle — a former patient — had asked, "How are you, doctor?"

Constable Bonsfield told the court that he had been on duty at Staindrop police station when Siddle said to him, "I suppose there's two men sworn that I have been threatening Smith?"

The constable hadn't replied, and Siddle had gone on to say: "I'll tell you what I've said many times, and I'll not deny that I have said that I should like to fight Smith whether I got three months or not."

Sergeant Daley testified that Lowson had appeared deeply affected when first questioned about the murder, asking with tears in his eyes, "Is he dead?"

This brought loud laughter from Lowson, sitting in the dock.

The three suspects were remanded in custody to await trial at Durham Assizes, where they appeared before Mr. Justice Hawkins on May 1st, 1884. Smartly dressed, they all pleaded not guilty to the charge of murdering the sergeant.

Two witnesses testified that they had seen Sergeant Daley find the pearl button at the scene of the crime. One of them was Dr. Middleton, who now found himself being

A couple of doctors were walking up this escarpment known as The Slack, when alerted to the policeman's fate

closely questioned about how much he had drunk on the night of the murder. He admitted he had been in a few pubs while he was in Bishop Auckland, but said he'd had only a glass of beer.

"Was that all?" asked Mr. Lockwood QC, defending.

"Well, I might have had a large whisky."

As laughter came from the gallery, the judge warned: "This is most unseemly. Three men are being tried for their lives. If I hear laughing again I will order the gallery to be cleared."

William Taylor, a workman from the nearby Raby estates, told the court that he had been present when the suspects were arrested. As they were being taken to the police station he had heard Lowson say to Siddle, "I hope we haven't murdered him, Bill."

Mr. Lockwood, seeking to show that both doctors had been drunk, and therefore

A local carter said he had seen Siddle approach a couple of policemen — one being Sergeant Smith — with a brick in each hand

incapable of identifying anyone or saying what had happened, called as a defence witness Benjamin Smedley, who had helped to remove the sergeant's body.

Smedley testified that he had at first refused to assist in carrying the sergeant, because the injured man had been placed on a door with his head too low, in a position which the witness thought might cause him further distress.

After Dr. Gorrick denied that he had heard Smedley complain, he was asked by Mr. Lockwood if it were true that he had been dismissed from his last post because of his drinking habits.

The doctor replied that this was not so: he had given in his notice. He admitted that he had fallen on his way to the Stag's Head, but denied that this was because he had been drunk.

Sergeant Daley testified that both doctors had appeared to be sober.

The final witness for the prosecution was George Hutchinson, a carter, who told the court that about seven weeks before the murder he had seen Siddle approach Sergeant Smith and Constable Knight with a brick in each hand. Hutchinson said he had shouted, "For God's sake, Siddle, lay down those

bricks!" and Siddle had walked away.

In his opening speech for the defence Mr. Lockwood said he would prove that the three defendants were home by shortly after 10.20 p.m. He claimed that both doctors had been "staggering drunk" and therefore in no position to make accurate observations. As for the button found at tne crime scene, it was very common, he contended, and could have come from the shirt of any one of those who helped to carry the sergeant away.

Mr. Lockwood went on to say that because Siddle had previously assaulted Sergeant

Smith the police had immediately assumed that he and his companions were the culprits. Working on that theory, the police had endeavoured to prove it — it was the foundation of their whole case.

As his first witness the defence counsel called Thomas Bell, a fitter with the North Eastern Railway. Bell testified that on the night of the murder he had seen Dr. Middleton and Dr. Gorrick at Bishop Auckland railway station. Both had appeared to be very drunk, Gorrick using disgusting language.

John Bentley, who was with Bell at the time, confirmed the

railwayman's account. And the barmaid at the Stag's Head said the two doctors had been boxing in the parlour. Both were drunk, and they had consumed three glasses of beer in a little more than an hour. Several other witnesses testified that the doctors had been the worse for drink.

One of Joseph Lowson's neighbours, Mrs. Elizabeth Simpson, said that the blood on his clothes had come from his daughter. About a fortnight before the murder the child had cut her lip badly. Mrs. Simpson had sent for Lowson, who had sat his daughter on his knee to attend to the wound. Blood was

Attackers had been drinking in this pub, the Royal Oak, when they spotted their victim, Sergeant Smith

pouring from the child's mouth and onto her father's clothes.

Dr. Rodway confirmed that he had visited Lowson's daughter, treating her cut lip. His assistant at that time had been Dr. Gorrick.

Siddle's brother Christopher told the court that on the night of the murder he had arrived home at about 10.20, his brother William arriving with Hodgson and Lowson about eight minutes later.

Hodgson's father, James Hodgson, refuted earlier testimony from Constable Donegan, who had alleged that Hodgson had intimated that he knew more than he was prepared to say.

Mr. Hodgson told the court that he had heard Donegan tell his son, "If you make a confession you will get a free pardon." When his son said nothing the constable had told him, "You are a silly boy not to tell all you know."

The defendant's father said his son had told him, "Father, I know nothing about it." Joseph had added that he had no animosity towards Sergeant Smith or any policeman, and he had harmed no one.

Mr. Hodgson went on to say that he himself had approached PC Donegan, asking if a confession from one or other of the suspects would "get them clear." He said Donegan had replied, "Yes, they would believe your son, but neither of the other two scoundrels."

In his closing speech for the prosecution, Mr. Skidmore said that he had expected great things from Mr. Lockwood after his opening address for the defence. But not a single link in the chain of

circumstantial evidence had been broken.

While deploring the defence counsel's attack on the doctors, Mr. Skidmore said that the prosecution did not care if they had been "as drunk as drunk could be" because the Crown's case did not rest upon the doctors' testimony alone but on that of

> ## "Because I threatened and assaulted Smith that does not prove I murdered him," said Siddle to the court

many other independent witnesses.

In his summing-up the judge told the jury that it was for them to decide whether one or all of the defendants were guilty, and whether the chain of circumstantial evidence was strong enough to convict any of the prisoners.

After deliberating for an hour and three-quarters the jury returned with their verdicts. There were cheers from the gallery as Joseph Hodgson was acquitted. William Siddle and Joseph Lowson were both found guilty.

When the convicted prisoners were asked if they had anything to say before they were sentenced Siddle told the court: "Nothing but lies have been spoken. If I swing, I am an innocent man. I never saw Lowson on the night of the murder ... because I threatened and struck down your victim and assaulted Smith, that does not

prove I murdered him."

Lowson, trembling and clinging to the dock, opened and closed his mouth several times before he could speak.

"I am innocent," he said. "The policeman Bonsfield will blush if he has to face me. He took my shirt and said there was a button off it. If the rope was around my neck I'd swear I never said a word in any shape or form. I have never said a word in the cells nor to anyone. There is not a man on the face of the earth can say I touched Smith, and have sworn my life away."

Donning the black cap, Mr. Justice Hawkins told the two that they had been rightly convicted of a cruel, cold-blooded and cowardly murder. "Without one single moment's hesitation or warning, you hurried him to his end, and

> ## The acquittal of Joseph Hodgson was greeted with cheers, and after the trial a crowd waited outside the court for him

without any provocation and for no other reason but that in the honest and faithful discharge of a very arduous duty he had excited your hatred against him."

"I had no hatred against him! I never said a wrong word against him!" Lowson protested.

Ignoring the outburst, the judge went on to sentence the two to death, urging them to "pray for pardon to the almighty God who alone has

the power to grant it."

"I want no Lord to have mercy on me!" Siddle shouted. Turning to the gallery, he continued: "They are a lot of — fools and thundering liars and perjurers. They have sworn away my life, lads."

He was then grabbed by warders who tried to bundle him down the steps.

Lowson too turned to address the gallery, shouting: "You will find out after, and when it's too late, that there has been nothing but perjury this day. I am an innocent man going down these steps, lads!" Cries of "Goodbye, hinnies!" were then heard as the two were dragged along the underground passage that led from the court to the prison.

Outside the court a large crowd had gathered waiting for Hodgson to be released. He emerged to loud cheers, looking pale, his boyish features drawn.

Asked by reporters to make a statement, he obliged. And what he was reported to have said sent shock-waves to the two men in the condemned cells. The reports said he claimed that he had been 200 yards away when Siddle and Lowson attacked the sergeant, kicking him to death. Later, however, Hodgson was to deny having said this.

Because of the circumstantial nature of the evidence there was strong public feeling that the sentences should be commuted to penal servitude

> ## The only one of the three to hang for the policeman's murder went to the gallows with a smile on his face

for life, and a petition to that end attracted thousands of signatures. An inquiry was set up, led by a commissioner from the Home Office. Hodgson, his father and the two doctors were among those questioned. Meanwhile a fund was established to assist Sergeant Smith's widow and children.

Back in Butterknowle, Hodgson wrote to Lowson saying he was sorry for him and Siddle and that he hoped they would keep up their spirits.

Lowson, annoyed and dismayed, wrote to his wife Jane, who was Siddle's sister. He said that Hodgson was "extremely cool," as it was he who had led the attack on the policeman.

DURHAM SPRING ASSIZES.

FRIDAY, MAY 2.

Before Mr Justice HAWKINS.

HE BUTTERKNOWLE MURDER.

SENTENCES OF DEATH.

e trial was concluded on Friday evening last of the
e men—JOSEPH LOWSON (25), JOSEPH HODGSON (20),
WILLIAM SIDDLE (25)— who were charged with the
al murder of Police-Sergeant Smith, at Butterknowle,
he 23rd of February last. The youth of the prisoners,
atrocity of the crime with which they were charged, and
peculiarly difficult evidence on which the prosecution
d for a conviction served to make the result a doubtful
and to concentrate around the case a widespread in
such as has seldom been exceeded. The best legal
stance was employed on both sides. Mr Skidmore and
Walton (instructed by Mr R. Richardson, of Barnard
le, on behalf of the Treasury), appeared to prosecut
le Mr Lockwood, Q.C., and Mr Greenwell (instructed
Maw, of Bishop Auckland), appeared for the defence. T
was commenced on Thursday morning se'nnight, i
caged court, and it may not be out of place briefly to
timate the proceedings of that day before proceedin
all the second day's proceedings. Mr Skidmore ope
case for the prosecution in an able and tempe
ech, which at once showed that he had thoro
tered the details of his case, and this was absolute
sential, and so much felt to be so that Mr Lockwood,
the trial, visited the scene of the crime, in order to
ore comprehensive understanding of the many imp
tails of locality which it was felt would certainly be
the course of the case. It was evident from t
ming remarks of the learned counsel for the pros
t the case against the prisoners who stood on
which lives rested entirely on a concourse of circum
ces, say one of which, standing alone, was of
of mine, but each of which forming a
o links in the chain connecting the acc
...ned against them. Summarised, th

Siddle claimed that Lowson could save him if he wished, but Lowson remained silent. Siddle then wrote a statement in which he claimed that he had arrived on the scene after the murder, and that Hodgson and Lowson were the culprits. This was handed to the prison governor, who sent it to the Home Office.

Learning of this, Lowson also made a statement. He claimed that Hodgson had struck the first blow with a stone, and that he had then joined in and they had killed the sergeant together. He said that he and Siddle had earlier agreed to make no statements while they thought they had a chance of a reprieve.

In a letter to his parents Siddle said he would not have been locked up for as much as a day but for others. "The result is I have to be hanged for another man ... instead of me being hanged for murder, I am going to be a murdered man." When relatives visited him in prison he told them that it was he whom the doctors had heard saying "Poor police, poor police."

Lowson wrote to his friend Ralph Blackett: "If they do right by Siddle they will send him home again ... Hodgson is the one that started it first."

Two days later Siddle was told that he was to be pardoned. Lowson, it seemed, would go to his death alone. He had always said he would rather hang than face life in prison, and as an atheist he shunned the prison chaplain.

When a piece of rope was found hidden in his cells and it was said that he had planned to commit suicide, he laughed, pointing out that as he was closely guarded night and day that would be impossible.

After his last visit from his wife and children he appeared depressed, but he soon regained his spirits and was again heard singing his favourite hymns — an odd repertoire for an atheist.

On the eve of his execution he read until ten o'clock and then slept soundly. Waking at 5 a.m., he washed and then put on the suit he had worn at his trial. He asked for bacon and a glass of ale for his breakfast. Both were provided, and he ate with relish. Sighing as he finished, he told the warders: "Now I am ready for them."

Berry, the executioner, had lodged at the prison overnight instead of at a local hotel as was his custom. He had checked the scaffold, ensuring that all was ready as Thomas Allison, the chief warder, went to Lowson's cell to escort him to the pinion room where Lowson laughed as Berry attended to him. He had been given a drop of eight feet.

On his last walk he smiled and nodded at those prison officers he knew as he passed them. "Is that the scaffold?" he asked as he approached it and then stepped firmly onto it.

Then, turning to the priest, he said, "Siddle is an innocent man, sir. Hodgson struck the first blow and I followed it up."

As the white cap was placed over his smiling face he shouted, "I hope that the country and Crown will look after Siddle and see they get him home safe again!"

Grasping the lever, Berry tried to pull it but it wouldn't move. He looked in surprise at a warder, who indicated that he should raise the lever. As he did so, Lowson shot through the opened trap-doors, to die instantaneously.

His dying wish subsequently came true when his friend and brother-in-law William Siddle was released from prison. What Siddle and Hodgson then had to say to each other was not recorded, and for the rest of Hodgson's life he was regarded by locals as a killer.

Siddle's freedom was short-lived. Certified insane, he was committed to an asylum, where he remained until his death.

There were dramatic scenes in Durham courthouse when one of the prisoners was acquitted – and the other two were sentenced to death

As THE personal friend of an executioner, William Johnson knew more than most about the fate that awaited a convicted killer. And that, as things turned out, was to make his own fate all the more extraordinary...

The 50-year-old farm labourer was

LANDLADY GUNNED DOWN IN HETTON-le-HOLE

a pal of the hangman William Marwood. He was also in love. For more than 17 years he had cherished the hope that one day his County Durham landlady would return his affection. But Margaret Addison, the 47-year-old widowed mother of four grown-up children, didn't want to know. To her Johnson was no more than a lodger.

As year followed year he reluctantly settled for biding his time...until 1890, when a rival came on to the scene.

Andrew Simpson, a 50-year-old miner, had been introduced to Margaret by her son Christopher, who worked alongside him at Hetton-le-Hole colliery. And it soon became painfully clear to William Johnson that within weeks Simpson had made more headway with the landlady than Johnson himself had achieved in years.

Like Simpson, he too had been a miner. Well-built and red-haired, he had come to the north-east from Horncastle in Lincolnshire—also the home of Marwood—and had worked at Unsworth pit for a year. Then after six years at Hetton-le-Hole colliery Johnson had returned to the agricultural work he liked best.

Now, 23 years later, he was the acknowledged champion hedge-cutter of the area. He had enjoyed this reputation for more than a decade, making a living touring farms in the district and doing whatever work they had to offer.

Since Simpson's arrival on the scene, however, there had been tension at Margaret Addison's home

"There'll be a funeral before there's a wedding!" So predicted William Johnson— champion hedger and a personal friend of hangman William Marwood—the day before he shot Margaret Addison to death outside her house in broad daylight...

at Four Lane Ends, Hetton-le-Hole, due to Johnson's obvious resentment. Finally the champion hedge-cutter was asked to find other lodgings. Oddly, however, he was still allowed to visit the house whenever he wished during the day. But for reasons that inflamed his imagination, he was no longer permitted to stay overnight.

He blamed Simpson for this, and his resentment intensified when he heard rumours that his rival and Margaret Addison were to be married.

On Thursday, October 29th, 1891, the extent of Johnson's anger became apparent to all at the Colliery Inn. Over drinks with railwayman friend John Cuthbertson, he complained that Margaret Addison still had some of his belongings and refused to let him have them back.

THE HETTON TRAGEDY.

SENTENCE OF DEATH.

At the Durham Assizes on Wednesday, before Mr Justice Wills, John William Johnson (40), farm labourer, was indicted for the wilful murder of Margaret Addison at Hetton-le-Hole on the 31st October.—Mr R. Luck and Mr W. A. Meek, instructed by Messrs Graham and Shophord, solicitors, Sunderland, appeared for the prosecution.

The prisoner on being placed in the dock presented the coolest demeanour. He is a strong, well-built, healthy looking man, and was well and neatly dressed for his class.

The indictment was read over to him, and on being asked the usual question as to being guilty or not guilty of the crime of murder, he without the slightest hesitation, and in a very firm voice, answered "Guilty, sir."

His Lordship: Johnson, you have pleaded guilty to

The pithead and screening belt of a County Durham coal mine. The unrequited love for a landlady was more than one ex-miner could bear...

Cuthbertson advised him to forget it, saying it would be better for all concerned if he left well alone.

Johnson was unmoved. "Look you," he told Cuthbertson and all those within earshot, "there'll be a funeral at the Lane Ends before there's a wedding!"

Cuthbertson told him to simmer down and not to be silly or things would only be worse for him.

"I'm not frightened of the rope," Johnson replied.

He was at his former lodgings again on Saturday, October 31st, and was busy sharpening his razor when Margaret's son Christopher walked in. The two ignored each other. Johnson blamed Christopher for Simpson's arrival on the scene; Christopher, aware of Johnson's resentment, had long since lost patience with the former lodger.

When he had finished shaving Johnson left the house, slamming the door behind him.

It was 8.30 a.m., as Margaret Addison saw when she looked at her clock. She must get a move on, she told herself, or she would miss her train. She was going to spend a week with her 86-year-old mother, who was finding it difficult to manage on her own. Margaret was hoping to persuade her to return to stay with her.

The landlady adjusted her new hat. Then, smartly dressed as always, she set out at 10 a.m. on her short walk to the station with her shopping basket in one hand, her umbrella in the other.

William Walker was busy doing road repairs as she passed. He looked up to catch her smile and cheery "Good morning."

Thirteen-year-old Sarah McCormick was just behind her. A

> **"I followed her and I did it. I came straight to the police station and gave myself up to Mrs. Cartwright. I also gave her the revolver that I did it with. I fired two shots at Mrs. Addison. I could stand it no longer"**

moment or two later the girl felt a tap on her shoulder. She looked up to see Johnson beside her, mumbling something she couldn't hear. Then she was horror-stricken to see him produce a revolver which he fired at Mrs. Addison's head.

The landlady put her hands to her head, crying "Oh, stop it!"

Johnson fired again. As she fell to the ground he approached her, looked at her for a moment, and then walked off briskly in the direction of the police station.

On hearing the first shot William Walker straightened up and looked around to see where the report had come from. Then he heard another shot and saw a terrified Sarah running towards him. Seeing Mrs. Addison lying in the road in the distance, he dropped his shovel and ran to her assistance, shouting to passers-by to fetch the police.

But Margaret Addison was beyond help. She lay face-down, her hair a mass of blood, her new hat lying a few feet away.

At the police station Sarah Cartwright was in her kitchen when Johnson walked in, asking to see Sergeant William Cartwright, her husband. The sergeant was out and not expected back for an hour, she said, so could Johnson call back then?

He looked at her for a moment, saying nothing. Then, "Mrs. Cartwright," he blurted out, "I have shot the landlady!"

Sarah Cartwright stared at him incredulously.

"Johnson, is it true?"

"Yes," he replied, handing her a revolver which she noticed was still warm.

"What else have you in your pockets?" she asked.

Without a word Johnson began to empty them, producing a penknife, a bunch of keys and three live rounds. She put them all in her husband's desk and then led him to a cell,

locking its door behind him.

On the sergeant's return he heard Johnson confess again. Charged with Margaret Addison's murder, Johnson was asked if he had anything to say. He replied: "I followed her and I did it. I came straight to the police station and gave myself up to Mrs. Cartwright. I also gave her the revolver that I did it with. I fired two shots at Mrs. Addison. I could stand it no longer."

Checking the revolver, Sergeant Cartwright found it contained two empty cartridges and four which had not been discharged. He handcuffed his prisoner and set out to escort him the two miles to Haughton police station. Most of the walk was made in silence, but as they neared their destination Johnson turned to the sergeant with tears in his eyes.

"I am happier now," he said, "than I would have been had she married him."

At the inquest which followed at the New Inn, Hetton, Christopher Addison confirmed that his mother had intended to marry Simpson. But he had never heard her quarrel with Johnson, he added.

St. Mary's Square, Horncastle, Lincolnshire. This was the home town of farm labourer and miner William Johnson—and of hangman William Marwood...

William Walker said he had spoken to Johnson shortly before the shooting, and at that time Johnson had seemed to be calm and collected.

Asked by the coroner if he could swear that Johnson had done the shooting, Walker shook his head. He had seen Johnson walking away afterwards, but had not witnessed

> **"It seems a plain and simple story. You were determined that the woman you shot should not be married to the man she was expecting to marry..."**

the shots being fired.

Dr. H. De Leigh testified that he had helped to conduct a post-mortem examination. He said this had found that the victim had been shot first from behind. That bullet wouldn't have killed her. It was the second shot that was fatal. This had passed through her left ear, destroying the most vital part of her brain, and her death had probably

been instantaneous. When her brain was removed during the autopsy the bullet fell to the base of her skull.

Although four more witnesses were waiting to be called, the jury passed a note to the coroner telling him that they had heard enough. They then returned a verdict of wilful murder against William Johnson.

Appearing before local magistrates the next day, he was remanded in custody to await his trial at Durham Assizes. This followed on December 2nd when in a firm, quiet voice he pleaded guilty.

"You have pleaded guilty to murder," said Mr. Justice Wills. "Do you appreciate the consequences? Do you understand what the consequence of your plea will be?"

"Yes, sir," Johnson replied.

"You have, I believe, been advised of your right to be defended?"

Two barristers were standing by in case Johnson changed his mind.

"My Lord, yes."

"You do not wish it?"

"No, I do not, sir."

To give him another chance to reconsider, the judge asked again: "You thoroughly understand what you are about?"

confession. Mr. Justice Wills refused the request. The confession would be sent to the Home Secretary, he said. It would be up to him whether or not it were made public. And that was the last that was heard of it.

Sleeping well on the eve of his execution, William Johnson awoke at 6 a.m. in Durham Prison on the appointed day, December 22nd, 1891. He dressed quickly, putting on the grey check suit he had worn in the dock. Breakfasting on toast and coffee, he then sat on a corner of his bed, patiently awaiting Billington, the hangman.

As the prison bell began to toll at 7.45 he began his 50-yard walk to the scaffold, his pace resolute, the

step of a proud man.

He had given all his belongings to Margaret Addison's family, and his sole visitor in prison had been a boyhood friend.

Billington had allowed a drop of six feet nine inches, based on the prisoner's 14 stone, muscular body. As the first chimes of eight o'clock sounded the executioner pulled the lever and William Johnson plummeted through the trap-doors. "Lord, to thee I commit my..." he had begun to say, but the sentence remained unfinished.

Rumours had meanwhile been circulating in Hetton-le-Hole. It was said that when Margaret Addison was shot she had actually been on her way to be secretly married. The stories were swiftly scotched by her family. Who could say whether the gossip had triggered the shooting? All that seemed certain was that sooner or later William Johnson would have acted as he did, determined to prevent the couple from enjoying the happiness that had been denied him.

"Yes," Johnson replied with a nod. The clerk of the court rose to ask if he wanted to say anything before he was sentenced. Johnson made no reply.

The judge appeared bemused. He was accustomed to protestations of innocence from killers who were obviously guilty, but this was his first encounter with a prisoner who apparently wanted to die.

"If I had been able to discover anything in the deposition," Mr. Justice Wills now told Johnson, "or in the circumstances of the case...that could have helped you, I should have impressed upon you the desirability of withdrawing your plea and pleading not guilty. But I think you have arrived at a just conclusion in thinking that an investigation could not alter in any respect the circumstances of the case.

"I am not surprised, although it is unprecedented in my experience that a prisoner should plead guilty to a charge of this nature involving the highest punishment of the law.

"I am not surprised it is so in this case. It seems a plain and simple story, odd as it is. You were actuated by jealousy, and you were determined that the woman you shot

should not be married to the man she was expecting to marry."

The judge then pronounced the death sentence...and Johnson calmly produced a piece of paper from his pocket and began to unfold it. Asked what he was doing, he replied he was going to read out his confession. The chief warder shook his head, telling him he had been given that opportunity and had refused it. Now it was too late.

In that case, Johnson replied, he wanted his confession to be handed to the press.

"Let it be handed to me," said Mr. Justice Wills. Then, after a cursory glance at the paper, he put it down.

Johnson, watching carefully, shrugged and left the dock without a backward glance.

Reporters covering the trial sent a message to the judge asking to be allowed to see the written

HE TA WAY T SCAFF

As the schooner *Lollard* slipped towards the quay alongside the Paillion Bottle Works, near Sunderland, the young ship's cook, Thomas Fury, was determined to be the first ashore.

Fury, who had signed on as Thomas Wright, wanted two things just then more than anything else in life – some beer and a bedmate.

The cash wouldn't be a problem – he had plenty of wages owing to him. He touched his cap to the captain, Albert Snaith, and said, "Please, sir, about my back wages ..."

A shipmate decided to join him on his shore leave

"Your wages can wait, Wright," the captain snapped back. "I've got more pressing things to attend to at the moment, like docking this ship."

"Where are you heading for when you get ashore, Tom?" Seaman John Lawrence asked Fury. They had been shipmates together on eight previous trips.

"I need a drink and a woman," replied Fury.

"I'll come with you."

With the *Lollard* safely tied up at the quay, Fury again pursued the subject of his wages with Captain Snaith.

This time he was paid up – the captain was to remember afterwards that it was a considerable sum.

Fury and John Lawrence clattered down the ship's ladder and headed towards the town. On the way they passed an ironmonger's shop. Fury went in, bought two knives, both with small, sharply pointed blades, and gave one to Lawrence.

"Just in case we hit any trouble, mind," he said.

First stop that night was the Wear Music Hall. After that they went to a pub. But Lawrence was already getting tired.

"I think I'll have one more drink then go back to the ship," he said.

"Aw, don't do that, John," Fury protested. "The fun hasn't started yet. We've got the whole night before us."

Lawrence wouldn't be dissuaded, though, and after finishing his pint he sloped out of the pub. Fury went part of the way with him and they parted company near Baines' Lane, a slum area in the nineteenth century that was home to most of Sunderland's prostitutes, thieves and hucksters.

As John Lawrence disappeared into the gloom towards the Lollard's berth, Thomas Fury drifted into Baines' Lane, whistling a sea shanty to himself and jingling the new sovereigns in his pocket.

What Fury did for the next few hours is unclear. But early next morning he was seen drinking in a Baines' Lane pub with a woman everyone in the district knew by name.

She was Maria

LKED HIS
O THE
OLD

Thomas Fury didn't much like the prison where he was serving 15 years for robbery. So he confessed to a murder of 13 years earlier – and made a date with the hangman

The *Lollard* in dock at Sunderland

Paillion Bottle Works dock, near Sunderland, where the *Lollard* berthed

Fitzsimmons, and at 31 she had risen to the dubious heights of the town's most celebrated prostitute. She was Irish, and the possessor of a fiery temper and the fastest thieving hands in the business. The shine of a sovereign put a glint in her eye, a glint that was bound to leave her client far worse off than ever he had anticipated.

Her nocturnal activities had put Maria in the dock at Sunderland magistrates' court no fewer than 23 times, on charges from disorderly behaviour to robbery. She was, said the town's police chief despairingly, a public nuisance.

Maria liked that. "I'm a public nuisance," she would boast to her clients. "But you should see what I can do in private."

After meeting Maria in the pub, Thomas Fury went home with her. At about 10 a.m. on Saturday, the day after the *Lollard* docked, she poked her head out of the tenement window, screaming "Murder!"

"Murder!" was a familiar cry in Baines' Lane. A few people looked up, most went on their various ways. But Maria persisted.

"Murder! Murder!" she shrilled.

At this a couple of neighbours with social consciences wearily climbed the tenement stairs. They found Maria in her room, clasping her throat and rolling her eyes dramatically.

Maria, of course, was bound to be robbing a client

"He tried to throttle me!" she yelled.

He, needless to say, was Thomas Fury, who had backed into a corner of the hovel and who now responded indignantly: "She's been tryin' to rob me ever since I got here. She's even nicked some of my clothes and hidden 'em somewhere."

The neighbours nodded sympathetically. They knew Maria. Of course she was trying to rob him. And with a few resigned shrugs they went off down the stairs again.

Three hours later, with Fury still in her room, Maria decided to go out and call on a girl friend named Wilkinson. Fury followed her and the girl named Wilkinson saw what happened next.

"Give us back my coat and socks," said Fury, "and I won't say nuthin' about the money you stole."

"All right," said Maria. She began to laugh happily. Fury kissed her passionately and they set off back to her room, holding hands.

The girl called Wilkinson wasn't to hear from Maria again, but the neighbours were. A few hours later they saw her poke her head out of the tenement window once again, and once again they heard the familiar cry.

"Murder!"

This time no kindly neighbours came to her aid, and only one person bothered to look up. He saw Maria alive and well. Thomas Fury could be seen through the window directly behind her, pulling her back, shouting at her to be quiet and not to be so silly.

That night, at about 10 o'clock, Maria had a visitor, a woman named Jane who lived in Monkwearmouth. Jane was paying a surprise visit to her friend, and when she arrived

she was surprised to find that although there was no answer from the door knocker, Maria's door was unlocked.

Jane opened the door and stepped into the room. It was in darkness, and unable to find any light, she went back into the street and found a mutual friend of Maria's, a girl named Nadia.

The two women got a torch and went back to Maria's room. The light revealed a pool of blood beside the bed; lowering the torch, they saw Maria's blood-soaked body under the bed.

She was sitting on the edge of the bed when she was struck

The prostitute's face was a mass of dried blood. Touching her they could feel she was cold and stiff. They ran out of the room and down the stairs, shouting "Murder!" at the top of their voices.

The call took a while to answer, for it had become an all too familiar cry in Baines' Lane.

When the coroner arrived he confirmed that Maria had been killed some hours earlier. She had ten stab wounds in her heart and two more in her back. She would have been sitting on the edge of the bed when the knife struck – a knife with a small, sharply pointed blade.

He put the body under the bed hoping it wouldn't be discovered

The stab wounds would have killed her almost at once. She fell back on to the bed, and then the murderer lifted her and put her underneath the bed, probably hoping she wouldn't be discovered for a while.

The room was in no more disarray than Maria might habitually have left it, except for a broken mirror which lay on the floor beside the bed.

Inquiries soon revealed that the last person seen with Maria was a sailor. The police issued a description of the man, but as a result of some confusing information, described him as an "Irish Yankee" sailor.

Police Inspector Elliot was despatched to London. His brief was to await the ships which had left port on the night of the murder and to see if any crew member fitted the description. He got there before the *Lollard* arrived and drew a blank on all the other ships. Dejected, he returned to Sunderland.

Three days after the murder, on Tuesday, 23rd February, 1869, an informant went into Manor police station in Sunderland and said the "Yankee" was hiding in a house in Bucks Row.

The police went to the house and arrested a man named Anderson, despite his protestations of innocence.

They had to let him go when the two principal witnesses, the girl named Wilkinson and the landlord of the pub where Maria and Thomas Fury had been seen drinking, failed to identify him.

While all this was happening, Fury had returned to the *Lollard* in his original persona of Thomas Wright, discarding his blood-soaked shirt in the River Wear on the way.

"How did you get those scratches on your face, Wright? " the mate asked him. "And there's a lot of blood on your trousers, too."

Fury laughed. "I was in a fight in a pub," he said. "The

other bloke got the worst of it, though."

He could see that the mate wasn't completely convinced, so when the *Lollard* arrived in the Port of London he decided to take the few days' wages owing to him and quit the ship for good. For the next two weeks he disappeared into the back streets and alleys of Victorian London.

On Saturday 20th, March, exactly a month after Maria's murder, Joseph Dyson went along to the Serpentine in Hyde Park for his daily dip. He had been bathing in the

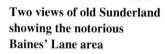

Two views of old Sunderland showing the notorious Baines' Lane area

Serpentine for more than 15 years, and it was his habit to go there early in the morning, when no one was about.

As he waded into the water, something floating caught his eye. It was a black pocket book, barely wet, so Dyson reasoned it couldn't have been in the water for very long.

Curious, he opened it and a wad of newspaper cuttings fell out. All of them were reports of the Sunderland murder. Then he began to read the pencilled handwriting in the notebook, and his hand shook with fright.

"I am the guilty one – and you will never catch me"

"I swear to you that the man Anderson is not the murderer of Maria Fitzsimmons," Dyson read. "He is innocent. I, the guilty one, will be on my way to America when this reaches you. You will not think to capture me because all the witnesses at the inquest gave the wrong description of me.

"Even supposing I had no more clothes to put on, nor any money to buy a disguise, which I have plenty of though Maria robbed me of 23 sovereigns, and blinded me an eye by throwing a looking glass at me which was found broken on the floor, you won't catch me. So I hope you will not shed innocent blood through me.

The prostitute had ten stab wounds in her heart and two more in her back

"I, the murderer, have been speaking to the witnesses in the case, and have not been recognised. I, the writer of this, am the murderer of Maria Fitzsimmons."

The notebook narrative then gave an account of the murder. The writer said he was robbed by Maria and had been woken up by her trying to strangle him. He decided to give the rest of the local prostitutes a warning, so he strangled her and then stabbed her.

The knife, he said, could be found hidden under the gate at Howden Dock in North Shields. And the note was signed "A MONSTER IN HUMAN FORM".

He wanted a reward for the murder he had committed himself

Dyson handed the notebook to the police, but there were no identifying marks on it and there was nothing they could do but enter it as an exhibit in a murder so far unsolved.

Then, suddenly, Fury surfaced. In Fleet Street he met a detective named Hann whom he knew. For Hann, Fury was a "copper's nark", a convicted thief who had on several occasions provided the detective with information leading to arrests.

Now Fury wanted to know if there was a reward for any information leading to the arrest of the Sunderland murderer.

Detective Hann said he wasn't sure, but he would inquire. Later he went back to Fury and told him there was indeed a reward, for £100.

"OK," said Fury. "I know who the murderer is, and if you'll be straight with me, I'll tell you where you can find him."

A waterman arrested at Wapping was completely innocent

"It's a deal," said Hann. "Come to my house and make a statement."

Fury declared that a man called Connor who worked as a Thames waterman was the murderer and, apparently with no more information than that, the police went in search of Connor. They found him at Wapping, and like the unfortunate Mr. Anderson, he, too, was arrested.

Despite his protestations that he had never even been to Sunderland in his life, let alone committed murder there, he was put up at the magistrates' court next day and remanded in custody.

Detective Hann, sure now that he had his man, alerted Sunderland police, who sent their Inspector Elliot on a second journey to London.

As he travelled south, Elliot must have felt like Sherlock Holmes, pulling together all the different strands of a complex case. For his inquiries in Sunderland after the *Lollard* left to sail to London had convinced him that the murderer had either worked or travelled on that ship.

In that case, who was this Connor?

The answer was soon forthcoming. Confronted with the unfortunate waterman, Inspector Elliot shook his head. "That's not the murderer," he said. "He doesn't begin to fit the description."

Angrily, Connor stormed off into the London streets, shouting over his shoulder that he'd sue the entire country's police force. Later, that was indeed what he did, receiving damages of £200.

Detective Hann hurried back to his informant. "No reward for you, Tommy," he said. "You got it all wrong about Connor."

"What makes you think that?"

"The cops in your home town sent down an inspector with a full description. Connor doesn't fit it. In fact, the inspector told me he thinks the murderer could have worked on a ship called the Lollard, which calls in at London every week and just happens to be docking tonight."

Tommy Fury visibly paled. The hunt for him was getting too close for comfort.

The captain remembered a seaman who quit the ship in a hurry

That night, as the *Lollard* came into port, Inspector Elliot and Detective Hann were waiting on the quay for it. On board, Elliot gave Captain Snaith a full description of the wanted man.

The captain shook his head. "We don't have any crewman who answers to that," he said. Then he thought for a moment. "There was a chap with us a few weeks back, name of Thomas Wright, who fits part of that description, but not all of it.

"And come to think of it, he did leave the ship rather quickly, a few days after that girl was murdered ..."

Detective Hann, of course, had no idea that Thomas Wright and Thomas Fury were one and the same man, and he had no idea either that Fury had worked on the *Lollard*. But he did have a friendly rendezvous arranged with Fury for later that night, and would in the ordinary course of events have described to his informant the conversation with Captain Snaith.

He was never able to do so because when he turned up at Fury's lodgings in the Suffolk Arms Hotel, the murderer had decamped. And for the next ten years Fury seem to vanish from the face of the earth, while the file on the murder of Maria Fitzsimmons, marked "Unsolved", gathered dust.

Then, in August 1879, a man named Charles Henry Cort was charged at the Old Bailey with robbery and attempted murder. He was found guilty and sentenced to 15 years.

Cort was moved from jail to jail until he was finally locked up in London's Pentonville Prison, in October, 1881, to serve out the rest of his sentence.

He wanted the world to know about his dreadful crime

Cort didn't like prison life, which in the last decades of the nineteenth century was harsh and extremely punitive. He was sure he'd never last 15 years, and the prospect of death itself was a happier one than the rest of his days spent in that gloomy, rat-infested institution.

So Cort asked the Chief Warder for a slate, and then scribbled down his story. He wasn't Charles Cort at all, he wrote; his real name was Thomas Fury. Thirteen years ago he had murdered Maria Fitzsimmons in her Sunderland room, and now he wanted the world to know about his dreadful crime.

When he handed in his slate he was called before the governor, who in turn called a prison director. So it was that on Friday 14th April, 1882, Thomas Fury appeared in the dock at Sunderland magistrates' court on a charge of wilful murder.

"I prefer to conduct my own defence," he announced, implying at the same time he would plead guilty at his trial at Durham Assizes. He asked the procession of witnesses a number of questions in cross-examination, then requested a day's adjournment to prepare still more questions.

When the prosecution objected, and the magistrates upheld their objection, the enigmatic prisoner told the court: "In that case I will have to tell a deliberate lie at the Assizes and declare myself not guilty instead of guilty."

At Durham 13 days later, Fury briefed a defence counsel, and he did indeed plead not guilty. The first witness to be called created something of a sensation.

He was Seaman John Lawrence, who had gone ashore with Fury on the evening before Maria Fitzsimmons was murdered. He told the court: "I am not aware that the prisoner is the same man with whom I visited the Wear Music Hall that night."

Then Lawrence was shown the black notebook found by swimmer Joseph Dyson at the Serpentine. He recognised it at

The Serpentine in Hyde Park in 1869, where a bather found a notebook containing Fury's confession

London docks in the late nineteenth century: here Inspector Elliot checked on all ships arriving from Sunderland

once. "It's mine," he said. "I had it with me on the *Lollard* and it disappeared from my locker."

Captain Albert Snaith had no doubt that the prisoner Fury was the man he knew as Thomas Wright, with whom he had made eight trips on the *Lollard.*

The prosecution's case was that Fury had shown knowledge of the murder and of Maria's room which was so detailed that only the murderer himself could have known.

The statement made by Fury was made at his own request. A celebrated handwriting expert, Mr. Chabot, had compared the writing in the black notebook and on the slate and declared that both were written by the same hand.

But, said the defence, there

Writing on the slate and in the notebook was by the same hand

was no reliable evidence to connect Fury to the murder.

"Fury is anxious to save himself from penal servitude, and because of that he has confessed to a crime of which he is not guilty. It is not the duty of the jury to assist him to commit legal suicide.

"There was no knowledge of the crime in his confessions that an intelligent man, as Fury was and is, could not have gleaned in

ordinary ways."

In any case, the defence argued, the man who killed Maria Fitzsimmons was guilty only of manslaughter and not murder, since he was acting to protect his property, so even if Fury were guilty, he would not escape penal servitude.

Frantic scramble as Fury threw a sheaf of papers at the pressmen

All this was rejected by the jury, who took only one hour to find Fury guilty of murder.

Fury didn't move a muscle when the verdict was announced. Asked if he had anything to say before sentence, he thumbed through a thick sheaf of written papers he had brought with him into the dock, and began a rambling statement which appeared to suggest he was the killer.

At length the judge, Mr. Justice Williams, cut him short. "Can you get to the point?" he asked. "How long is this going to take?"

Fury cleared his throat and began again. After a few minutes more the judge stopped him again, this time for good.

Fury looked helplessly towards the press box, shuffled together the sheaf of papers, and threw the lot at the pressmen. A frantic scramble ensured as everyone

tried to catch them.

Put together after the trial was over, the bundle of papers constituted a rambling account of the life of Thomas Fury, sailor.

"My father was a drunkard, and my mother forced to become one," Fury had written. "The poor woman was held down by relatives as they poured rum down her throat until she promised to be more friendly.

"As for me, I was a raving drunk before I'd reached my eighth birthday and repeatedly drunk by the time I was ten."

Drink, he said, was the only purpose in life for many seamen. As he grew up he began to understand that alcohol gave him an irresistible urge to cause injury to others who had given him no provocation.

Of the 13 years out of the last 18 he had spent in prison, he had only ever met one prisoner whose crime was not carried out while he was under the influence of drink.

But before all this was made public, the judge, donning the black cap, made it clear that he wasn't happy with Fury's behaviour during the trial and especially with the paper-throwing incident.

"You have been found guilty of what seems to be the most atrocious and diabolical murder I have ever dreamt of," he said. "It was a crime you confessed to yourself, and it was only owing to anxiety on my part to be certain of the truth of that confession that I determined it

should be tested by sworn testimony.

Hoped trial had been long enough to satisfy the prisoner

"Everyone present, even yourself, must be convinced that you have had a thorough, exhaustive, and most patient trial which I hope, without being too long, has been sufficiently long to satisfy everyone, even yourself."

Fury was then sentenced to death. As he was being led away he stopped and turned slightly, as if about to say something. Then he thought better of it and disappeared down the steps.

Less than three weeks later, on Tuesday 16th May, he awoke in the condemned cell for the last time and ate breakfast of toast, jam and tea.

Would he have preferred penal servitude to oblivion? Did he in his last few hours on earth regret the confession that took him inexorably to the gallows? If he did, he said nothing. He walked to the scaffold unaided and was hanged at 8 a.m.

It was an extraordinary price to pay to escape a prison sentence.

The End of a

"WE ARE all in all to each other. I belong to Ruth and she belongs to me and she knows it," Thomas William Shelton told one of his girl friend's colleagues. "If I don't get her no one else will. I'll do her in, and she knows it. I'm not afraid of the consequences."

The unemployed engineer's courtship of Ruth Surtees Rodgers had been far from easy. They were both 25 and she had been his girl friend for six years, four of them as his fiancée. But for a long time Ruth's mother had refused to have him in the family's Abbey Street home in Gateshead.

Mrs. Rodgers objected to his attitude, his temper and his behaviour towards Ruth, but on New Year's Day in 1924 she relented, acknowledging Shelton at last as her daughter's "intended" and allowing him into the house.

A few months later Ruth got a new job in Pink Lane, Newcastle, as a confidential clerk with the City Floorcloth and Linoleum Company. Her boss there was the fatherly Walter Shiel, a 45-year-old married man with three children. Ruth's father had died in 1917, and she soon found herself turning to Shiel for advice, not least about problems with her fiancé.

As the months passed Shelton began to notice a cooling in Ruth's attitude towards him. Then on November 15th, 1924, she removed her engagement ring. This passed without comment from Shelton, but he could hardly have failed to notice it. He began to suspect that the office manager Walter Shiel was responsible for the change in Ruth, and that Shiel was poisoning her mind against him.

Shelton began taking days off work when he would follow Ruth as she left home for Newcastle, and back again when she left her office. He was seen hanging around Pink Lane and he started recording Ruth's movements in his diary.

By December he was increasingly on edge, and when the couple attended a Christmas dance there was a distinct coolness between them. This was noticed by Ruth's friend and colleague, 21-year-old Ruby Banns. Shelton seemed to be in a foul mood and the pair hardly spoke to each other. Ruby took Ruth aside and asked what was the matter.

Ruth shrugged and said she hadn't been ready when Shelton called for her. Shortly before the dance ended Shelton took Ruby to one side, asking her which club Ruth was going to on Friday nights. Ruby told him she'd no idea—she didn't even know Ruth was going to a club. At work the next day Ruth showed her friend a letter from Shelton. Ruby saw that it was full of threats and accusations.

Shelton actually hired a private eye to spy on Ruth, and the investigator knew that his client was unbalanced

On Christmas Eve Shelton took his washing to the laundry where he beckoned the manageress Hannah Quigley, whom he knew well. He told her that he believed his girl was "knocking around" with another man. Miss Quigley told him not to worry, saying, "It'll all sort itself out." Shelton told her that if he couldn't have Ruth, no one else would.

As soon as the Christmas holiday ended he went to see John Trotter, a Newcastle private inquiry agent. He told the investigator that he believed his ex-fiancée was attending a secret women's society which met every Friday night at different places. He had seen Ruth leave such a meeting, he said, and she had then met a man. Now he wanted her to be followed.

Noting that Shelton had a wild look about him, Trotter suspected he was mad. He advised his caller to go home and think it over. If he still felt the same the next day he could come back and then they would see what could be done.

Trotter also suspected that

Gateshead seen from the Newcastle end of the High Level Bridge (below); the setting for a passion-driven murder. and the High Street seen from Jackson Street (right)

Sweet Romance

DOUBLE EXECUTION AT DURHAM

Shelton wouldn't be able to afford his fees, but in that respect he was wrong. Shelton had lost an eye in an accident at work when he was a 16-year-old engineering apprentice, and he had received substantial compensation. From this he had paid £70 into Ruth's bank account after they began courting.

He went to Ruth's workplace again on January 24th. Turned away, he stormed out of the building shouting his suspicions of Walter Shiel.

Four days later Ruth's elder sister Georgina was going to catch a tram in Gateshead when Shelton approached her. "Have you seen Mr. Shiel this morning?" he asked.

She ignored his question and they walked along Durham Road in silence. Then he suddenly stopped and shouted: "Don't keep it back! I know you've

seen him! He telephoned you yesterday and fixed an appointment—it's no good trying to deceive me, for I know!"

"I'm not trying to deceive you or keep anything back," Ruth's sister replied.

"What are you going to do about this business?" Shelton persisted, referring to his suspicion that Ruth's lover was Shiel.

"I will have to hear both sides of the story," Georgina answered, "before I can decide."

They walked a little further. Shelton stopped again as they reached the Town Hall. "If I don't get her no one else will," he said, handing Ruth's sister two letters. "Read these."

The first letter was in Ruth's small, neat handwriting. "Dear Tom," it said, "It must be plain to you that things have not been as they should for some

considerable time, and it has therefore come to this: that in the interests of us both we should part, as I have repeatedly told you that I should never marry you."

The letter then continued in capital letters: "THIS WILL BE

SUFFICIENT REASON SO THAT YOU MAY LOOK TOWARDS SOMEONE ELSE TO SHARE YOUR COMPANIONSHIP. We shall of course part friends. Nothing more can be said, as I am

DOUBLE EXECUTION.

Men Hanged Side by Side at Durham.

FATE MET WITH COMPOSURE.

Coroner Graham's Criticism of Capital Punishment.

A double execution took place in Durham Gaol this morning, when Thomas Henry Shelton, aged 25, fitter, of Gateshead, and Henry Graham, aged 42, window cleaner, of Sunderland, suffered the extreme penalty of the law for sweetheart and wife murder, respectively.

INQUESTS ON THE BODIES.

Veteran Coroner on His "Gruesome Work."

Alternative to Hanging.

The inquests on the two bodies were held later in the morning within the prison. The inquiries were conducted by Mr. John Graham, Coroner, and Mr. John Hall was foreman of the jury.

Formal evidence was given by the Deputy Under Sheriff, Mr. A. A. Luxmoore—who was present in court when the men were sentenced to death and also at their execution —by the Governor of the Gaol (Colonel Hales), and by the prison surgeon, Dr. [...]

foreman, the last named [...]
[...] given to

From the time he had sliced his sweetheart's throat until the time he was hanged for it, Thomas Shelton positively cavorted with joy. As the papers reported, the Wearside man was as happy as a skylark

determined to choose and keep my own friendships."

The second letter was also from Ruth: "Just a short note to let you know we are finished at 1 p.m., so I will wait until you come down."

Georgina handed the letters back to Shelton without a word.

"I think Mr. Shiel has a hold on Ruth," he said.

"How can that be?" asked her sister. "Don't you know he's married, with three children? Don't worry about him—he's just taken an interest in Ruth as he has no man friends. Mind

"I've done her in," boasted Shelton from the middle of the road, where he continued to shout until the door was slammed...

you, if there had been a man in our house you would not have dared to take advantage of her as you have done."

"She's not wearing her engagement ring," Shelton continued.

"I'm not surprised—you've had it back so many times. I've often said that if she was me I'd throw it at you!"

Shelton began weeping as he replied: "She has said to them in the city, 'What would you think if you heard of me being murdered?'"

An hour later he was at Ruth's workplace, sharing his troubles with the firm's book-keeper William Pearson. Asked if Ruth had said why she had broken her engagement, Pearson replied that she hadn't spoken of it. Shelton again claimed that Shiel was her lover, saying he had seen a letter the office manager had sent Ruth signed "Walt."

Meanwhile Ruth's mother had become increasingly worried. Shiel had arranged to

see her to explain that he and Ruth had only a working relationship, although he had accompanied her on several occasions because she said she was terrified of Shelton and what he might do to her.

At 5 p.m. Georgina and her mother set out to keep their appointment with Shiel. On their return they found Ruth and Shelton together, both apparently in high spirits. Catching Georgina's eye, Shelton nodded towards her music book which lay on the table. She glanced at it and saw a piece of paper protruding from its pages.

Picking up the book, she saw that the paper was a note from Shelton: "Ruth says there's another chap, so if you get at her about it I shall see you sometime where it will be all right. Please state on the bottom of this tonight."

"I don't think she will say anything to me," Georgina wrote in reply. "But I will see you on Friday night."

To the relief of her family, Ruth seemed to have enjoyed her evening with Shelton. But early the next morning Shelton shared his grievances with a tram conductor, Charles Taylor, who was about to start his second journey of the day when Shelton boarded his tram. By the time the talkative stranger alighted the embarrassed conductor was glad to see the back of him, deciding he was "wrong in the head."

By 10 a.m. Shelton was at the laundry again, telling Hannah Quigley what Ruth was getting up to. Showing the laundry manageress a razor, he said that he knew what he had to do. Shocked, she told him not to be so silly. He returned the razor to his pocket and left hurriedly. At 4 p.m. he was back in Pink Lane waiting for Ruth to leave work. When Ruby Banns came out 20 minutes later he asked where Ruth had got to and he was told she had already left.

He asked Ruby: "Do you know if she has someone else?"

Not wishing to become involved, Ruby shook her head and said she must go, as her mother was waiting. Shelton gripped her arm, saying he had asked Ruth to marry him but she had refused. "I'm wretchedly miserable," he went on, "and I can't sleep or even work. Ruth's on my mind all the time."

Ruby excused herself and hurried off.

Ruth's neighbour Beatrice Scarth was returning home with

her weekly shopping when she saw Ruth with Shelton, who had his arm round the girl's shoulders. A moment later Mrs. Scarth saw Ruth break away and run across the street with Shelton in pursuit. Ruth screamed and struggled as he grabbed her and drew his hand across her throat. Mrs. Scarth looked on in horror as Ruth then tottered a few steps and collapsed outside her own front door. Shelton fell on top of her. Both were moaning softly.

Eleanor Vest, Ruth's married sister, was upstairs cleaning when she heard someone hammering at the front door. She was half-way down the stairs when she heard someone moaning. She opened the front door to see Ruth lying with her head on the step, covered with blood. Shelton, also bleeding from the throat, was now standing in the middle of the road. "I've done her in!" he shouted.

As Eleanor and Mrs. Scarth carried Ruth inside, Shelton continued to shout "I've done her in!" until Ruth's front door was slammed behind her.

The Rodgers' next door neighbour Mrs. Annie Carr was listening to her radio when she too heard someone thumping on her front door. She opened it and Shelton staggered in. "I have killed Ruth," he said.

Bewildered, Mrs. Carr asked: "What with?"

"A razor," Shelton replied, adding that it was still somewhere in the street.

Mrs. Carr took him into her kitchen, sat him down and went to fetch a doctor and a policeman. Shortly afterwards the police surgeon Dr. Stanley Robinson responded to an urgent message calling him to Abbey Street. Examining Ruth, he found her to be dead: her jugular vein totally severed.

Next door he found Shelton sitting calmly in the kitchen. The doctor examined his throat wound, found it to be superficial, dressed it and awaited the ambulance he had summoned.

Arrested on his way to Newcastle Infirmary, Shelton was placed under a police guard at the hospital pending his appearance before Gateshead magistrates.

A further development was revealed at Ruth Rodgers's resumed inquest on February 12th when her sister Georgina told of her conversation with Shelton in Durham Road the day before the murder.

When Georgina said that

Shelton had asked if she had seen Mr. Shiel that morning the coroner interrupted. Turning to the jury, he said: "I may tell you that Mr. Shiel cannot be called as a witness as he is suffering from something which has obliged him to be where this man"—indicating Shelton— "has come from. I mean Newcastle Infirmary."

Walter Shiel had lost his job, moved from Newcastle to Whitley Bay, and attempted suicide.

As Georgina continued to testify the coroner stopped her again. "I am not going to put this on the depositions," he told the jury. "This man who is not able to attend and this sister were acting as friends of both sides. It is rather an awkward position when two people fall out to try and get friends to patch up the matter. This is what it means. There was nothing in it. Shiel did his best."

The inquest concluded with a verdict naming Thomas Shelton as Ruth's killer.

Further evidence exonerating Shiel was heard when Shelton appeared before Gateshead magistrates less than a week later. Mr. Frank Lambert, prosecuting, told the court of Shelton's suspicion that Ruth and Shiel were having an affair. But the prosecutor went on to say: "In point of fact Mr. Shiel was taking a friendly interest in Ruth, as she had told him plainly on several occasions that she was terrified of Shelton and that she really did feel that he might try and take her life as he had previously threatened to. He had interested himself so much in the girl that he had even seen her mother to try and explain to her her daughter's fears...it was not unreasonable that he constituted himself as the girl's guardian, given his age and his position in the firm."

Shelton's solicitor Mr. Barry Jones sought to show that his client had been insane at the time of the murder. To this end he questioned the doctor who had treated Shelton on his arrival at hospital. What had been Shelton's state of mind?

"He appeared unusually cheerful and most certainly showed no concern over his actions," the doctor replied.

But the court heard that before Ruth's death Shelton had appeared to be under great stress. William Pearson, the book-keeper where Ruth was employed, testified: "I had the impression that he was not altogether responsible. He had a wild look about him and he seemed both nervous and excited."

Walter Shiel also appeared nervous as he stepped into the witness box. He had earlier been in the dock charged with attempting suicide, and that case had been adjourned.

He told the court that he had spoken to Shelton on only two

on to say that he understood that Shelton's defence would be insanity at the time of the murder.

Mr. Archibald Wilson, defending, then called the laundry manageress Hannah Quigley. Saying that she had known Shelton for some time, she told the court that she observed a definite change in him when he showed her his razor.

Further defence witnesses described Shelton's stressed state prior to the murder, and Walter Shiel was then called to testify.

He had paid Ruth Rodgers no more attention than any other girl in his charge, he told the court.

"Is it not a fact," asked Mr. Wilson, "that you have taken the girl out on more than one occasion?"

object in it. It was just because she felt the cold and needed a scarf," said the witness, adding that he had not been aware that Shelton resented the attention he paid the girl.

"Is it not a fact that you have attempted to commit suicide?"

Walter Shiel turned to the judge. "My lord, have I to answer that?"

"Is this really necessary?" Mr. Justice Acton asked the defence counsel, who said he would not press the issue further.

Inspector Moore, who had been called to the scene of the crime, told the court that a diary and four letters had been found in Shelton's possession when he was arrested. Two of the letters were read out. Both were to Shelton's mother, the first telling her that they would meet in heaven, the second asking her to see that he and Ruth were

anything to say before he was sentenced, he shouted: "Shiel's the trouble! That's the man!"

He then heard the death sentence passed, snapped to attention, turned smartly about in the dock and disappeared down the steps to the cells.

His appeal dismissed and a petition signed by thousands disregarded by the Home Secretary, he was informed of the death of his mother as he awaited his execution. This took place on Wednesday, April 15th, 1925, when Durham Prison saw its first double hanging for 17 years.

Shelton woke early and put on the new blue suit he had bought for his trial. Then he had a good breakfast and sat and waited for the hangman, Thomas Pierrepoint. His companion on the scaffold was to be Henry Graham, a 42-year-old

Gateshead High Street, circa 1925. The inhabitants were becoming accustomed to hangings for murder in their town

occasions. The first was when he had been to a meeting in Gateshead. As he was about to depart in his car he had met Ruth quite by chance and had given her a lift home. On the second occasion Shelton had come up to him and had asked, "Are you a married man?"

At the conclusion of the hearing Shelton was remanded in custody to await trial at Durham Assizes. Appearing there before Mr. Justice Acton on March 25th, 1925, he smiled wryly before he pleaded not guilty to Ruth Rodgers's murder.

Opening for the prosecution, Mr. G.F. Mortimer KC outlined the facts of the case and went

"Never—with the exception of going in the car," Shiel replied.

The same judge had tried the man who would be Shelton's companion in death: a window-cleaner who had murdered his wife

"Did you ever on more than one occasion lend Ruth a scarf—and why?"

"There was no sentimental

buried at a time and date which he had previously requested.

Dr. Robert Stuart, a prison physician, testified that Shelton had shown no sign of insanity while he was in custody.

In his closing speech for the defence, however, Mr. Wilson contended that Shelton's behaviour both prior to and after Ruth's death indicated that he was not responsible for his actions. "After the girl had broken off their engagement a change had overtaken him and jealousy had been eating at his heart."

After 75 minutes' deliberation the jury returned to find Thomas Shelton guilty. Asked if he had

Sunderland window-cleaner who had been tried in the same court before the same judge.

Graham had murdered his wife, and throughout their time in the condemned cells the two men had been kept apart. Shelton, unaware that Graham had declared himself happy as a skylark, often sang in his cell to keep up the spirits of his unseen companion.

The brief meeting of the two on the scaffold, with a fate in common and spending their last moments alive together, was strangely silent. Not a word was exchanged. Then the lever was pulled and it was too late.

THE MOMENT his 30-year-old wife was granted 15 shillings a week maintenance and a separation order in August 1924, Henry Graham resolved never to pay it. Margaret Graham's five-year marriage to the 42-year-old window-cleaner had become increasingly unhappy. Now she had left their home in Wear Street, Sunderland, taking their five-year-old adopted son with her to live with her mother two miles away in Rutland Street.

Her husband's first letter begging her to return to him arrived a week later. She ignored it, together with all the others that subsequently came from him. He'd change his ways, he promised. Later letters threatened what he would do to her if she didn't come home. She became increasingly worried and began taking extra care when out on her own.

From time to time Henry nevertheless managed to accost her in the street, renewing his pleas for her to come back to him. On each occasion she refused. She'd never return, she told him, advising him to pay the maintenance order before he found himself in prison.

On Sunday, December 21st, 1924, she had arranged to visit her sister Elizabeth, a patient for several months in Sunderland Infirmary. Elizabeth's husband Robert Dolman was also due to visit her, together with her cousin Matthew Swan, who was on holiday in Sunderland from his home in Ellesmere Port, Cheshire.

Henry Graham also made for the hospital that afternoon, waiting nearby for his wife to emerge at the end of visiting time. When Margaret, her brother-in-law and her cousin left the infirmary they made their way along St. Mark's Road deep in conversation. Robert Dolman was pleased to have been told that his wife might be able to return home during the coming week. None of them saw Henry Graham bearing down on them.

"I want an explanation," he said to Margaret, at the same time indicating that her two companions should walk on. As they did so slowly, they heard the couple arguing. Margaret again refused to return to her husband. "There's no more to be said," she told him, trying to push past him.

Saying he had bought a knife for their son, Henry Graham reached into his pocket. With his other hand he punched her in the face. She fell to one knee, wiping blood from her mouth. Graham then produced a sheath from which he withdrew a knife, stabbing her three times in the back and the arm.

She cried out and managed to get to her feet. As she ran across the road her husband grabbed her, stabbing her a further seven times. She collapsed, semi-conscious and losing blood.

Robert Dolman heard her scream and ran to help her. He stopped as Graham, waving his knife wildly, warned him to keep his distance. Henry Graham then fled up the road, pursued by John Robson and Charles Jenkins, who had witnessed the attack.

Running up Duke Street, Graham turned into Hilton Street. Looking over his shoulder he saw the two men gaining on him, followed by a small crowd of men who had taken up the chase. In Hilton Street Graham suddenly stopped and leant against a wall, panting.

"Where's the knife?" Robson asked him.

"Here it is," Graham replied, proffering it blade-first.

"Turn it around," Robson ordered.

Graham stared at him for a moment and then surrendered the knife, handle-first, as Jenkins joined them.

"I will tell you all about it," Graham volunteered. "It was my wife and we have been separated for four months. I wrote to her to try and make it up, but she wouldn't come back. I told her the consequences and it is done."

"You will get the rope for this," said Jenkins.

"Yes. I can't help it," Graham replied. "Get a policeman."

The pursuing crowd arrived and formed a circle round him, a few kicking and punching him. Seeing the crowd, Detective Constable Thomas McManus hurried down the street to investigate. Robson handed him the bloodstained knife and told him what he thought Graham had done. The officer saw that there was also blood on Graham's hands.

"I bought the knife for the kiddie," Graham told him. "We've been separated for four months, and I met her in the street today. She wouldn't come back on any terms, so I stabbed her in the back. I meant to do it and I hope she's dead."

McManus asked him where the attack had taken place.

"I expect she'll be lying at the bottom of the street now," Graham replied. "I will take you to where I did it."

Margaret Graham's screams had also alerted two patrolling policemen. Constable Good was the first on the scene, finding that the stabbing had taken place opposite his own front door. He turned the victim face-down in an attempt to stem the blood pouring from her back. Cutting away her blood-soaked clothes, he tried to bandage her wounds, at the same time sending someone for an ambulance. He then helped to carry her into a nearby house. As he placed her on a couch she said, "Harry did it!" before she lost consciousness.

Henry Graham arrived escorted by McManus, who hustled him into the house as an angry crowd had gathered. On seeing his wife, Graham kissed her on the cheek. When this was witnessed by some of the crowd peering through the window they tried to force their way inside to get at him.

Margaret Graham and her

"I met her in the street today. She wouldn't come back on any terms, so I stabbed her in the back. I meant to do it and I hope she's dead"

husband were then put in an ambulance. Taken to the hospital which she had left hardly an hour earlier, she died shortly after her arrival. For his own safety her husband was kept in the ambulance and taken to the police station.

On the way he said to McManus, "I hear she's dead. Is that right?"

The detective said this was so.

"It's a good job," Graham continued. "I know where she is now. I won't be long following her. I expect I'll get this." Pointing to his neck, he indicated an imaginary noose.

At the police station he was charged with his wife's murder. "Yes, that's right, sir," he replied.

Meanwhile the victim's blind brother had arrived at the scene of the attack as the crowd began to disperse. Told what had happened, he decided to delay informing his mother as she was bedridden, suffering from heart trouble.

At Margaret Graham's inquest the next day her cousin Matthew Swan said he had never seen her husband before the afternoon of the murder. He had walked on a few yards after Henry Graham accosted his wife and had then turned round to see Graham holding a brown sheath

DOUBLE EXECUTION AT DURHAM

King George V at Pickersgill Yard, Sunderland, in 1916, and the bridge just below the shipyard. Eight years and a few streets away Margaret Graham was granted 15 shillings a week maintenance and a separation order against her window-cleaner husband...

"I Won't Be Long Following Her"

from which he took a knife, plunging it into Margaret three or four times as she knelt on the ground. Graham had then fled, pursued by others in the street who had been alerted by Margaret's cries.

Inspector Cook testified that when he met Graham in the charge room, Graham said: "Good afternoon, Mr. Cook. It's come at last." After being cautioned he had

said: "I am not going to deny it. You know the life I have had. I went up the street and met her today. I had a scout knife I had bought for the boy. I asked her to take it and she refused. I stabbed her in the back with it."

The inspector added that when he went to see Margaret Graham's mother to tell her what had happened she gave him a bundle of letters sent by her son-in-law to her

daughter.

Dr. Cookson, who had conducted a post-mortem examination, said that Margaret Graham had received 10 stab wounds, three of them severe enough to kill her. The one which had caused her death through massive blood-loss and severe shock had traversed the muscles in her back, penetrating her diaphragm.

Without leaving the courtroom,

the jury returned a verdict of wilful murder against Henry Graham, who was remanded in custody.

His trial before Mr. Justice Acton at Durham Assizes took place on March 6th, 1924. Chewing gum, he pleaded not guilty.

Outlining the case for the prosecution, Sir Henry Cautley KC, MP, said that the knife Graham had used had a six-inch blade. He asked the jury to consider whether anyone would be likely to buy such a knife for a five-year-old child. In conclusion, he said that he understood that the state of Graham's mind would be raised by the defence. But there was no evidence, he told the jury, that Graham was insane.

The court then heard from Dr. Robert Stuart, medical officer at Durham Prison, where Graham had been under his observation since December 30th. The witness said that the prisoner had shown no sign of insanity. Although it was possible that he had been insane at the time of the crime, it was highly unlikely.

Both Robert Dolman and Matthew Swan told the court that Graham had appeared to be sober when he stabbed his wife. Under cross-examination, Dolman said the prisoner had acted like a lunatic, but Swan said he believed that Graham had known what he was doing.

No witnesses were called for the defence, but Graham's counsel, Mr. G.H. Wilson Fox, submitted that his client's demeanour at the time of the crime showed him to have been of unsound mind.

Henry Graham, standing stiffly to attention and still chewing gum, appeared unmoved when the jury found him guilty. Asked if he had anything to say before he was sentenced, he replied: "I thank you for your verdict. I also can say that I have got satisfaction and I have also kept my word, sir, and got my wish. As a man I say, 'A life for a life.' I am highly satisfied with the verdict."

Sentenced to death, he saluted smartly and as he turned to leave the dock he paused to glance at the public gallery. Seeing a man overcome with emotion, he called, "Hello, Jack." He then threw a piece of paper to another person, but a warder was ordered to return it to him.

At the Appeal Court on March 30th Graham's counsel told the Lord Chief Justice that his client had been blown up at St. Eloi in 1915 while serving in the army, and this had helped to unhinge his

mind. Mr. Wilson Fox went on to say that it was useless to gloss over Graham's admissions, but at the time he had not known what he was doing.

Dismissing the appeal, the Lord Chief Justice said it was based upon faint supposition which was not supported by the evidence. Graham had been calm and sober when questioned by the police.

The condemned window-cleaner took the news of his appeal's failure calmly, hoping instead that a reprieve might result from a petition to the Home Secretary.

There was no reprieve, however, despite the petition's 10,000 signatures. Nevertheless Graham told visitors that he was "happy as a skylark." Meanwhile his mother had died, her death accelerated—it was believed—by the stress of her son's predicament.

Warders enjoyed the cheerful prisoner's jokes, and when friends paid their final visit he told them he had never felt better, urging them not to be afraid for him as he would go briskly to the scaffold without fear. He also said that he had been given a bottle of beer a day, and when he was later asked if he wanted anything in the form of a stimulant on the morning of his execution he replied: "Yes, it will put still more spirits in me."

He had been eating well, and during his time in the condemned cell he had gained nearly a stone and a half. Telling his brother not to grieve for him, he said he was looking forward to rejoining his wife.

In a double execution on Wednesday, April 15th, 1925, he shared the scaffold with Thomas Henry Shelton, a 25-year-old fitter from Gateshead who had cut the throat of his girl friend. The two exchanged no words as they stood side by side on the trap-door, and both were reported to have gone calmly to their hanging, carried out by Thomas Pierrepoint and William Willis.

Graham, reading his Bible until the executioners came for him, had walked firmly to the scaffold repeating "Oh, lamb of God, I come," over and over again.

The double execution was followed by inquests on the hanged men, the coroner, Mr. John Graham, saying he had lost count of the number of times he had officiated at such inquiries after bodies had been taken from the pit beneath the scaffold.

He recalled that there had been a time when "the poor wretches

ascended a ladder, and at the top they were allowed to make a dying speech to their friends and admirers. The hangman's work was to place a slip-knot around the man's neck. The ladder was then pulled away from under the man's feet and he was left dangling."

The time had also passed when people went to executions as though

Sunderland Infirmary (right). An hour after visiting her sister here on December 21st, 1924, Margaret was on her way back, this time as a patient. Below, Sunderland station and Brougham Street market a few years after the tragedy

to a football match, to see the last writhings of the wretches who were hanged. There had also been other improvements in the way hangings were conducted, and he sensed and welcomed a change in public opinion with regard to executions in general.

Turning to the question of a substitute for the death penalty, the coroner said: "Put a murderer behind bars so that he cannot get out, and let him remain there for the rest of his life. But do not go through the farce of penal servitude for life, and then after he has earned so many marks let him out again."

There should be no chance of remission, Mr. Graham continued, and in cases where there had been abominable cruelty "the cat" was a very useful implement. "There should be something in addition to penal servitude for life before the eyes or knowledge of the person who is going to commit a murder,

they were alive, of being shut away from all the pleasures of this world, it might prevent them. It is worth a trial.

"I know there are objections, and one of them is a contemptible one and not worth thinking about—the expense. People who think in terms of pounds, shillings and pence will say, 'Why should we pay for the cost of keeping them in prison for life?' But when we deal with the question of £.s.d. can we shut our eyes to the dole? The money wasted on the dole would keep all the murderers

Above, part of the newspaper report on Coroner John Graham's outspoken views. The time he had passed when people went to executions as though to a football match, he said in part...

DOUBLE EXECUTION.

Men Hanged Side by Side at Durham.

FATE MET WITH COMPOSURE.

Coroner Graham's Criticism of Capital Punishment.

A double execution took place in Durham Gaol this morning, when Thomas Henry Shelton, aged 25, fitter, of Gateshead, and Henry Graham, aged 42, window cleaner, of Sunderland, suffered the extreme penalty of the law for sweetheart and wife murder, respectively.

Both men walked with steady steps to the scaffold, and last night Graham told some friends that he was " as happy as a skylark."

Conducting the inquests, Mr. John Graham, the veteran Coroner, delivered a strong criticism of capital punishment, and advocated as an alternative penalty, imprisonment for life, without any remission of sentence.

It is 17 years since two men were hanged together at Durham, and on that occasion the murderers were J. T. Noble and Robert Lawman, both of Gateshead.

either at present in existence or for some time to come. It would keep them safe, and you would get better value for your money."

A letter in a periodical at the time had said that more and more people were revolting from the whole conception of capital punishment, which as a deterrent in cases of murder had demonstrably failed, the coroner concluded. "I am certain that the system of hanging is not going to last, and the sooner it ends the better for everybody."

Posterity was to prove him right, though there are still many who would argue that the ahead-of-his-time coroner had got it all wrong. What is beyond dispute, however, is that if Mr. Graham's words had been acted upon, with life imprisonment meaning precisely that, numerous double killers would have been prevented from murdering a second time.

DURHAM TRAGEDY

SUNDAY BREAKFAST was a leisurely affair at Mrs. Bryan's small boarding-house in County Durham. The house in Parker Terrace, Ferryhill, catered for working men, and as Sunday was their day off the meal was unhurried, with time for conversation.

"I had a strange dream last night," Mrs. Bryan remarked as she served breakfast on Sunday, February 12th, 1928. "And it was about you," she told one of her lodgers.

"Well, if it was about me it must have been a nightmare," laughed William Byland Abbey, a 31-year-old cashier at a local bank.

"Yes," Mrs. Bryan continued, "I dreamt you were attacked at work and murdered!"

"That's odd," said Abbey, "because *I* had a dream like that last night. I dreamt I was being murdered — my attackers tried to quieten me but they couldn't kill me. They got hold of my throat and I felt a terrible sensation of choking. They came for me two or three times and I couldn't get away ... but it was only a dream, after all."

"Fancy that!" said Mrs.

remember for the rest of her life.

On February 16th Mrs. Edith Dyke had some bills to settle. It was 3 p.m. when she entered the Ferryhill branch of Lloyds Bank. She saw a tall man leaning over the counter, talking to the cashier. She heard the customer say, "I'll go and see if he is coming." He then left the bank.

When Mrs. Dyke followed him out a few moments later, with her money tucked away in her purse, she noticed that the tall man was standing outside looking up the road. As she left he went back into the bank.

Bending over his work at the counter, William Abbey looked up ... too late. A terrific blow to his head rocked him backwards, but he kept his balance and grabbed his attacker as four more blows rained on his head, knocking him to the floor.

THE FERRYHILL BANK AND THE PREMONITION

Bryan's young daughter Elizabeth. "We're having breakfast with a man risen from the dead!"

Abbey got up from the table, his arms outstretched, and began to wail as he imitated a ghost.

"What would you do, Billy, if you were ever attacked?" asked his landlady.

"I'd pick up my brass weight," Abbey replied, "and throw it straight through the window. There's always people outside and that would attract their attention. The attacker wouldn't get far ... but it'll never happen."

The talk at the table moved on to other subjects. Nobody gave it another thought ... until four days later, when that Sunday breakfast became something Mrs. Bryan would

As he struggled to his knees he saw the glint of a blade which grazed his jaw. Then the knife struck again, severing the main artery in his neck. He nevertheless managed to haul himself up from the floor again by grasping the counter. He fumbled for the brass weight used to weigh coins, found it and hurled it through the window before he sank back to his knees.

The sound of the glass shattering stopped passers-by in their tracks. John Heavisides looked round to see a tall man walking quickly away. Thomas Armstrong, also

nearby, saw a man come from the bank and make off towards Durham Road.

The crash of glass was also heard by William Kell, who ran into the bank, to find Abbey sitting on a tin box, covered with blood and barely conscious.

Kell asked who had attacked him.

"A tall man," Abbey gasped, "who's just left."

Heavisides had meanwhile

run to the police station. Constable Philip Grieves had passed the bank only minutes before. He now dashed back, followed by Sergeant George Fleming.

Abbey was still sitting on the box at the end of the counter, trying to stem the blood pouring from his neck and pooling at his feet. "It was a tall man who did it," he repeated in response to Grieves's questions. "He took

DID THE MAN H

Ferryhill's main thoroughfare photographed in 1928

would then take the money to the Spennymoor branch.

At 3.40 p.m. a bus left Ferryhill on time. It stopped at a metal bridge on the outskirts of the village to pick up a young man who flagged it down. The conductress felt sure she'd seen him at Ferryhill bus station at about 2.30, but as she chatted to him he said he'd not been in the village.

The passenger alighted at Coxhoe, where he was seen by another bus driver, John Butterfield, who knew him by sight and spoke to him. Butterfield later remembered the encounter because the young man had looked dishevelled, whereas he was usually smartly turned out.

That afternoon Tom Wetherall was on duty in the porters' lodge at Sedgefield Mental Hospital. He looked at the lodge clock in surprise when he saw Norman Elliott, a 23-year-old male nurse, walking up the drive. It was 4.50, and Elliott wasn't due to

JOB
F DEATH

FERRYHILL BANK TRAGEDY.

Elliott Declares Another Man Committed The Crime.

REMARKABLE STATEMENT.

Interest in the Ferryhill bank crime was strongly revived yesterday when, at the Courts, Durham, before Mr T. F. Brass, O.B.E., and other justices, Norman Elliott, aged 23, an attendant, lately employed at the Durham County Asylum at Sedgefield, was brought up, after three formal remands, on a charge of the wilful murder of William Byland Abbey, aged 31, cashier at the sub-branch of Lloyds Bank at Ferryhill.

The affair, still fresh in the public mind, occurred on Thursday afternoon, February 16 and evoked a sensation throughout the country. On the fifth day after the commission of the crime, while thousands were paying their tribute to the memory of Mr Abbey at his funeral in Ferryhill, Elliott

BANK MURDER APPEAL FAILS.

Ferryhill Sentence To Stand.

"HOPELESS" GROUNDS

Elliott Hears Decision Without Emotion.

NORMAN ELLIOTT, the young attendant who was sentenced to death at Durham Assizes for the murder of William Byland [Abbey], cashier of the Ferryhill

go on duty until 9 p.m.

He went into the building and emerged half an hour later. He was back again at nine o'clock to report for his shift, and as he passed the lodge he asked Wetherall if he had heard anything about the Ferryhill murder. The porter said he had only heard rumours.

Another male nurse, Lockhead, was surprised to see Elliott approaching him on his ward. Elliott owed him money, and had been avoiding him — he had collected Lockhead's wages for him a week earlier, but had failed to hand them over, making the

Norman Elliott (right) had been married only a month when the crime was committed

everything."

A few moments' silence followed. Then he whispered, "I am going …" and he died minutes later.

Questioning potential witnesses who crowded into the bank, Grieves received conflicting accounts. Some spoke of a tall man walking briskly away. Others said they had seen a well-dressed man leave the bank, pause to button his overcoat, and then

walk to a chocolate-coloured Rover parked about 50 yards down the road. He seemed to have trouble starting it, but had then driven off at speed.

A black-handled cobbler's knife lay in the pool of blood, and cash missing from the bank totalled £202 15s. 8d. A cheque made out for a substantial sum had also been

taken.

It had been Abbey's practice at around 3 p.m. to count the day's deposits, marking the notes with his signature in pencil and recording the amount. He

CALLED SINCLAIR REALLY EXIST?

In this pretty church Norman and his wife were married

excuse that he had left Lockhead's wage packet in Durham.

As days passed and Lockhead began to suspect his wages had been spent, he had threatened to report his colleague to the police. But now it seemed he had worried unnecessarily, for Elliott came up to him and handed him the £3 2s. 10d. owing. Elliott offered no explanation and Lockhead didn't ask for one — he was simply relieved to get his money, and to find that his suspicions had apparently been unfounded.

Those doubts about Elliott, however, had been natural enough. He earned only £2 7s. a week, from which £1 3s. was deducted for his board and lodging at the asylum, leaving him only £1 4s. to support the pretty nurse he had recently married and who had since become pregnant — she was still living at the Turk's Head Inn which her parents managed at Kelloe, for the young couple could not afford a home of their own.

The next day Elliott invited his colleague Patrick Kelly into his room where he showed him a new pair of brown boots which he said he'd just bought for a pound. He then opened his wardrobe to display a new suit and overcoat, for which he said he had paid £4 10s., proudly showing Kelly the receipts for all the purchases.

The following day Elliott was off-duty. He had recently arranged to rent two rooms in a house near Kelloe colliery, so he went to meet his wife, with whom he planned to buy furniture for their new accommodation.

His mother-in-law commented on how smart he was looking in his new blue suit, mauve overcoat and brown boots. But she wondered how he had been able to afford them — her daughter had complained that he was giving her only £1 2s. a week to live on, and she received that only intermittently. She had recently written to him, "The next time you come, for

Young Elliott left himself only two shillings a week after paying his board and lodgings and giving his wife half his money

goodness sake bring some money, as I cannot live on air."

Meanwhile the owner of the brown Rover parked near the Ferryhill crime scene had come forward. He had been in the village on business, he said, and he was eliminated from the inquiry when it was established that he had left at least half an hour before the murder.

Superintendent Frederick Foster, leading the investigation, turned a deaf ear to demands from the public that Scotland Yard should be called in. He was confident that the killer would soon be caught without outside assistance.

On February 20th the laundry mistress at Sedgefield asylum was inspecting the washing when she noticed a particularly dirty shirt in Elliott's pile. When she saw bloodstains on the right cuff she went to the matron and they called the police.

Superintendent Foster arrived at the asylum to learn that Elliott had left at 6.15 that morning. Two officers remained to guard the suspect's room while Foster went to Spennymoor, where Elliott was believed to have gone to lay linoleum at his new home.

Once again the wanted man had departed by the time the police arrived. Having completed his job at his flat, he had caught a bus to Kelloe.

This time Foster got ahead of him. With other officers he was waiting in Kelloe when the bus arrived, and Elliott alighted, to be told he was wanted for questioning. Taken to the Turk's Head, he was asked to account for his movements on the day of the murder.

"I wasn't at Ferrryhill at all on that day," he insisted.

Told that witnesses had seen him in the village and outside the bank, he admitted that he had been in Ferryhill but said he had not been near the bank.

He was then taken back to the asylum where he was asked to unlock the drawers in his room. He couldn't do so, he said, because he didn't have the keys with him.

"Then we'll force them," one of the officers told him.

He quickly produced the keys, and a search of the first drawer revealed 63 ten-shilling notes wrapped in a blanket. That accounted for £31 10s. of the bank's missing money. Eighteen bloodstained one-pound notes and 11 ten-shilling notes were also found, and a further £21 9s. 9d. came to light when Elliott turned

out his pockets. The cash recovered now amounted to £175 18s. 7d., and heavily bloodstained clothes were discovered in a portmanteau.

Asked to account for the money, Elliott claimed that some of it had been left to him by his deceased father, some of it he had saved, and the rest had been won through betting on horses and football.

"I am not guilty of that," he replied when he was charged with Abbey's murder.

His arrest coincided with the victim's funeral in Ferryhill, where a crowd estimated at 6,000 gathered for the service held round the war memorial. The mourners were told that away from the bank William Abbey had been an accomplished Baptist lay-preacher and a talented composer whose operetta *Vala* had been performed several times in Durham. As the final hymn began his fiancée collapsed, sobbing uncontrollably.

At the inquest Mr. R. V. Dickinson, representing 30,000 members of the Bank

LINGFORD'S BAKING POWDER

The Durham Chronicle AND COUNTY GAZETTE

No. 5635. Established 1820. FRIDAY, FEBRUARY 17, 1926.

DARING BANK ROBBERY.

Cashier Murdered And Money Stolen.

VICTIM A DURHAM CITY MAN.

A brutal murder which appears to have been carefully planned and deliberately carried out, caused consternation in Ferryhill Village yesterday afternoon.

The victim was Mr William Bayland Abbey, aged about 30, clerk in charge of the local branch of Lloyds Bank, who is a member of an esteemed family in Durham City.

When Mr Abbey was found he was dying, but before he expired from terrible wounds he was able to gasp "A tall man did it."

After securing about £200 in notes the murderer decamped, and search is being made by the police for a visitor to the village who was seen to leave the place in an old Rover car of a brown or chocolate colour.

Mr Abbey had been felled with some blunt instrument and stabbed twice in the neck, and an important clue is a cobbler's knife, bearing an American trade mark, which the murderer left behind.

A shout from inside the bank about 3 p.m. first directed attention to the crime. A minute later a well-dressed man, a stranger to the neighbourhood, emerged, and, walking at an ordinarily brisk pace to a waiting motor car, boarded it and drove away.

About a minute later there was a crash of glass, and a brass weight fell on to the pavement outside the bank. This was the last despairing effort on the part of Abbey to draw attention to his dire predicament. It is obvious that after getting his injuries and the departure of the murderer he picked up the weight and hurled it into the street to attract attention.

Four men—William Kell, Joseph Vickers, Thomas Armstrong and John Pearson—who were standing in the street near the bank, at once ran across the road and entered. There they saw Abbey staggering behind the counter with blood streaming from him. He collapsed almost at once, and died in the bank within a quarter of an hour.

enter. The man's description is:—About 5ft. 10ins. in height, about 30 years of age, figure smart and erect; clean shaven, fresh complexion, dressed in a brown suit—the jacket tight and smart fitting—light cap, collar and tie.

"Entered the bank carrying an overcoat on his arm, but was wearing the overcoat when he left the bank shortly afterwards.

"The injuries inflicted indicate that the deceased was struck four or five times on the head with some blunt instrument, probably from the front of the counter. Later he was stabbed twice in the right side of the neck with a new cobbler's knife with round black handle stamped 'Made in U.S.A., South-bridge, Mass.'

"It seems inevitable from the nature of the injuries that the assailant's clothing must have been considerably bloodstained, and he covered these stains by putting on his overcoat.

Marked Treasury Note.

The bank where the murder occurred, showing in centre the door through which the wanted man entered.

Mr Abbey was the second son of Mrs Abbey, of the Mount, Gilesgate, Durham, and the late Mr Charles Abbey, his father being a draughtsman at Messrs

The hole in the Bank window which Mr Abbey made by hurling a brass weight in his dying efforts to attract attention.

Front page news in *The Durham Chronicle* showing crowds gathered outside the bank, the victim William Abbey, and the window he managed to break

than the bank clerk, but that Mr may have made a strenuous resistance gathered from the scuffling and shouting that took place within the bank before the murderer was seen by several men to take up his coat and walk quietly away to the waiting car.

Beyond the fact that he was a well-dressed man, and obviously town bred

front, dickey seat.

"The police are anxious to trace a person and a car answering these descriptions, and they will appreciate information of such a car seen on the roads after 3 p.m., and the direction in which it was travelling.

"They are also anxious to trace where the knife described was purchased, and would be glad if persons coming into

Officers' Guild, told the court that a similar tragedy in Borden, Kent, had prompted the coroner's jury to condemn bank branches staffed by only one person, in view of the danger to which such cashiers were exposed.

Mr. Dickinson said it should not have taken another murder to alert banks to the seriousness of the situation and to persuade them to do something about it.

A Lloyds Bank spokesman told the court that the Ferryhill branch was in a very public place, "entirely surrounded by glass, and if anyone had suspected that a murder could take place there, common-sense would have said it was impossible."

Wearing his new suit and overcoat, Elliott appeared before Durham magistrates on March 15th, when the prosecution claimed that he had been in Ferryhill both on the day of the murder and the day which preceded it, "to enable him to make his plans and watch how the bank operated."

The court heard that he had spent money freely during the weekend after the murder. One of his friends testified that Elliott had flashed a large roll of banknotes, saying: "Wouldn't you like to be as I am, and buy a new top coat?"

The prosecution alleged that in a statement Elliott had said: "I did no murder, but am aware of the identity of the person who did it — namely, a person I know as Sinclair."

The grandson of a police inspector and the son of a constable, Elliott had claimed that he had first met Sinclair in the South of England more than a year ago, on a charabanc going to Hurst Park racecourse.

"On the journey to the course I found this man Sinclair to be an entertaining and most agreeable companion and well up on his knowledge of racehorses and all things pertaining hitherto and other sport in general.

"I told him who I was and he said, this being my first trip to town, he would be pleased to meet me any time so long as he was able to get down to the Sandown Park meeting the

following day. When we arrived on the course he advised me to pay two or three shillings above the ordinary course fee to get a better place of access for him.

"Just before the big race he came up and told me to back Kinnaird as it was a certainty. It was eight to one in the betting. I put my hand in my hip pocket to extract a note, but found it had been picked and I had lost a bundle of ten one-pound notes. I said I would go to the police and report it, and Sinclair told me I was in London and should be a lot sharper."

In his statement Elliott went on to say that he put £2 on Kinnaird to win, and it did so at six to one. He then repaid a loan from Sinclair, who did not want to accept it. It did not occur to him at the time that Sinclair had picked his pocket.

The statement then described backing winners at Lincoln, Elliott claiming that by the end of his holiday he had trebled the money he set out with — thanks to Sinclair, with whom he had continued to keep in touch.

Sinclair subsequently had business to attend to in Ferryhill, Elliott's statement continued. Sinclair told him to wait for him outside the bank,

It never occurred to him, said Elliott, that Sinclair was the one who had picked his pocket. At least he won some of his money back

where he would be about five minutes before closing-time to cash a cheque. On passing the doorway Elliott had seen Abbey standing inside, doing something with a telescope. They exchanged remarks on the weather, and Elliott asked if his friend had called. Abbey said he had not, adding that the friend would have to hurry up because it would soon be three o'clock and he had to catch a bus.

Elliott's statement claimed that he then went to look for his friend. He couldn't see him, and when he returned to the bank at five-past-three he was surprised to find it closed, as Abbey had said he would wait a few minutes before he locked up.

Elliott said he tried the door, it swung open, and he was pulled inside by Sinclair, whose hands and jacket sleeves were covered with blood. Sinclair threatened dire consequences if Elliott raised an alarm. He then stuffed a bundle of notes into Elliott's pocket and told him to clear out and say nothing, as he would be brought into the crime if Sinclair were arrested.

In his statement Elliott said he then stood petrified, but on hearing a groan he went to the counter and saw Abbey huddled up. He put his overcoat on the counter and rushed round to help the cashier, but he thought he had died. He intended to remove the knife which was protruding from Abbey's neck, but when he touched it the bank clerk gave a groan. Elliott said he lost his nerve, put on his overcoat and gloves, left the bank and went back to the asylum. But he couldn't settle, so he had later gone by bus to Coxhoe before his shift began that evening.

He had intended to count the money and then send it to the police anonymously, but the sight of it had sent him into a cold sweat and he had decided to hide the banknotes until he had the courage to burn them and his bloodstained clothes.

After Elliott's statement had been read, the prosecution called three witnesses who testified that they had seen him outside the bank shortly before the murder.

It seemed strange that Elliott could not say where Sinclair lived, even though he had received several letters from him

Mr. H. E. Ferens, prosecuting, told the magistrates that they might think it strange that Elliott had been unable to tell the police where Sinclair lived, although he claimed he had received several letters from him.

The day before the murder, the prosecutor continued, Elliott had been so hard up that he was wearing shoes that were totally worn out — he had stuffed paper inside them,

and only this was keeping his feet from contact with the ground. He had closed his account at the bank six months earlier and "had no right at all to be there from a business point of view."

Committed for trial at Durham Assizes, Elliott pleaded not guilty when he appeared before Mr. Justice McKinnon on June 26th, 1928.

Opening the case for the Crown, Mr. G. F. L. Mortimer KC told the jury that after shopping in Stockton for furniture, clothes and other items Elliott had sat next to the conductor on a bus, producing a wad of banknotes and saying, "How would you like to pay bills like that and have money when you are married?"

The prosecutor continued: "A number of notes found in his possession were notes that had passed through Mr. Abbey's hands, and at

least a number of them were stained with Mr. Abbey's blood. If you reject the story which he has put forward that these notes were thrust into his hands by the man Sinclair, what possible explanation can there be but that it was his hands that killed Mr. Abbey?"

The court then heard medical evidence that Abbey had received five rapid blows to his forehead from a mallet or light hammer. These would have knocked him unconscious. The first attempt to stab him had been foiled by the blade striking bone, but the second was fatal.

"It must have been a very determined attack?" asked Mr. Mortimer.

"A very determined attack," Dr. James Jack confirmed, "and it was meant to kill."

For the defence, Mr. Arthur Linsley asked: "It would require a man of great strength to inflict these injuries?"

"Not necessarily of great strength, but of great determination," the doctor replied.

Under cross-examination Sergeant Fleming admitted that neither Mrs. Dyke nor a grocer's errand boy who had both noticed a tall man at the

One good thing occurred as a result of the murder of William Abbey — and that was that one-man banks ceased to be, and staff security was improved

80

bank just before the murder had been able to identify Elliott as the man they had seen.

"Of fourteen witnesses at the identification parade," Mr. Linsley told the jury, "only eight picked out Elliott, four didn't and the other two didn't really want to."

Superintendent Foster said that inquiries had been made throughout the country in an effort to trace the man named as Sinclair in Elliott's statement. Photographs had been obtained of 124 known racecourse thieves who might have used the name Sinclair as an alias, but on being shown these Elliott had failed to find the man he had described. Instead he picked out a man whom he claimed had been with him and Sinclair at Lincoln on March 21st, 1927.

"The man," said the superintendent, "couldn't have been in Lincoln on that day as he was safely locked up in Durham Prison!"

Stepping into the witness box, Elliott repeated his claim that the murder had been committed by the man he knew as Sinclair.

"When you saw the body of Mr. Abbey, you knew what Sinclair had done?" asked Mr. Mortimer.

"Quite."

"Did it not occur to you to inform the Ferryhill police?"

"He had threatened to pull me into it."

"How could he pull you into it?"

"His word was as good as mine."

"Suppose you had gone straight away and given the hue and cry?"

"I hadn't time to think of that."

"There were people outside in the street," remarked the judge.

"Quite so, my lord," said Mr. Mortimer.

Concluding the case for the prosecution, Mr. Mortimer told the jury that it was clear that Elliott had no money before the murder but afterwards had been able to spend freely, and his story concerning Sinclair was "so incredible that it could only have been invented in those circumstances by a man who himself was an actor in the crime."

For the defence, Mr. Linsley reminded the jury that several witnesses had failed to identify Elliott, who had never been in trouble before but was claimed by the prosecution to have suddenly conceived the idea of committing murder and robbing the bank — an act which could only have been committed by "a savage, ferocious beast."

Furthermore, said the defence counsel, Elliott and Abbey had lived near each other and knew each other. So if Elliott were the killer, Abbey would surely have recognised him and named him instead of speaking only of a "tall man."

Summing up, the judge said that in considering Elliott's story the jury must ask

Wouldn't Abbey have named Elliott as his attacker, since he knew him well, if in fact Elliott *was* the man who had attacked him?

themselves if Sinclair existed. He added that notes undoubtedly taken from the bank had been found in Elliott's possession, and his clothes were bloodstained. If that evidence stood alone, it could point to only one conclusion.

After a short retirement the jury returned to find Norman Elliott guilty. As he was being sentenced to death his jaws began working, and as the final words of the sentence

STORY OF SINCLAIR.

124 Photographs Collected By Police.

FERRYHILL TRIAL.

COUNSEL AND ELLIOTT'S ALLEGATION.

Does The Man He Called Sinclair Exist?

JUDGE'S SUMMING-UP.

"TOOL OF SINCLAIR."

Man Who Never Gave an Address.

MURDER GOING ON, BUT NOT A NOISE.

Assailant Narrowly Misses Being Caught Red-Handed.

FERRYHILL DISCLOSURE.

Policeman Passes Door At Time Of The Deed.

STORY OF A DIRTY SHIRT.

Garment The Head Laundress Handed To The Police.

DEATH SENTENCE PASSED ON ELLIOTT.

Dramatic Ending To Bank Murder Trial.

ACCUSED COLLAPSES IN COURT.

Frenzied Cry of "Oh, Mother, Mother, Mother!" from the Dock.

NORMAN ELLIOTT, the 22-year-old Sedgefield Asylum attendant, was sentenced to death at Durham Assizes, this afternoon, for the murder of William Byland Abbey, clerk-in-charge of the Ferryhill branch of Lloyd's Bank, on February 16.

On hearing the sentence accused collapsed in the arms of four warders. He recovered, and, as if in a frenzy, cried out: "Oh, Mother, Mother, Mother!" The scene was one of intense poignancy.

Mr. Justice MacKinnon, in his summing-up, laid emphasis on the fact that no one had seen the man named Sinclair, whom Elliott had stated was the perpetrator of the crime.

It was also difficult to understand, he added in effect, why accused, when pulled into the bank by this man Sinclair, did not call for help when he realised his position. It was for the jury, briefly, to believe or disbelieve Elliott's story.

UNCANNY COURT SILENCE.

Condemned Man's Sister Carried From The Gallery.

were pronounced he threw back his head and cried: "Oh, Mother! Mother! Mother!" Then he collapsed into the arms of the warders beside him. His cries continued to be heard as he was dragged away along the passage beneath the court. Meanwhile his sister collapsed in the court's public gallery and was carried out.

His appeal dismissed, Elliott spent much of his time in the condemned cell gazing at photographs his wife had sent him of herself and their son. The child had been born while Elliott was in custody and had been named after him.

There was no reprieve, and on Friday, August 10th, 1928, Norman Elliott was hanged at Durham Prison.

His widow had been his bride for little more than a month before his arrest. She subsequently remarried, and William Byland Abbey's death proved not to have been in vain. It lent weight to his fellow-cashiers' campaign to put an end to one-man banks, and that end duly came.

LONG BEFORE Neighbourhood Watch, Newcastle had something equally effective: neighbourhood nosiness. Residents of Mitford Street, Elswick, had little opportunity to do anything unobserved, as John William Anderson discovered on August 28th, 1875 ...

Although he had trained as a clerk, Anderson seldom stayed long in the same job. He had also worked in the local shipyards and had a brief spell in the army, from which he persuaded his wife Elizabeth to buy him out as he couldn't stand the discipline.

Elizabeth was 29. To support her 32-year-old husband and their two sons she ran a small grocery in Mitford Street. The couple's elder nine-year-old boy didn't get on with his father and had been sent to London to live with friends of the family. The younger son, seven-year-old William, remained at home.

It took Elizabeth a year's scrimping and saving to scrape together enough money to buy her husband out of the army. She should have known better.

Two views of Scotswood Road, Newcastle. Alcoholic John William Anderson spent most of his time in the pubs in this street — there were then 54 to choose from — and indeed he was drunk on the night he murdered his wife

King's Meadows shipyards off Elswick. Anderson worked here for a time, but he seldom held any job for long

he had told Danskin there would always be a place for him in his home, and Danskin had taken up the offer on leaving the army in 1873. He and his wife had become the Andersons' lodgers, Bridget helping Elizabeth in the shop.

The Andersons seemed to be in good spirits that evening, and the Danskins — aware of the couple's increasingly strained relationship — were pleased to see this. But trouble loomed when Anderson mentioned that he had seen Bridget Garratt in Gateshead that day. This was the woman Elizabeth suspected of having an affair with her husband.

"Yes, it is her you should be with," she told Anderson.

Ignoring her, he continued his conversation with Danskin. Meanwhile Elizabeth told Bridget she couldn't stay any longer. She must lock up the shop, she said, asking Bridget to help her.

Bridget agreed, but Anderson had other plans. Telling Bridget to stay where she was, he asked Elizabeth to fetch him a quart of beer.

Shaking her head, Elizabeth said

Neighbours eavesdropping on the Andersons heard slapping noises, shouts, abusive language and the sounds of something being dragged across the floor. This was all rounded off by two blood-curdling screams ...

He spent most of his time in the pubs — there were 54 to choose from on Newcastle's Scotswood Road alone — and when his money ran out he helped himself to things from the shop to pay for his ale.

He was an alcoholic, and he was becoming violent. The couple's rows became more frequent, but they

nevertheless went out drinking together on the evening of Saturday, August 28th. It was 9 p.m. when they decided to return home. Elizabeth had to lock and shutter the shop, but they first saw Benjamin Danskin and his wife Bridget.

Anderson had known Danskin for five years. Meeting him in the army,

EWCASTLE MURDER

"I A WHORE?"

NEIGHBOURS HEARD ELIZABETH SCREAM SECONDS BEFORE SHE WAS BRUTALLY MURDERED

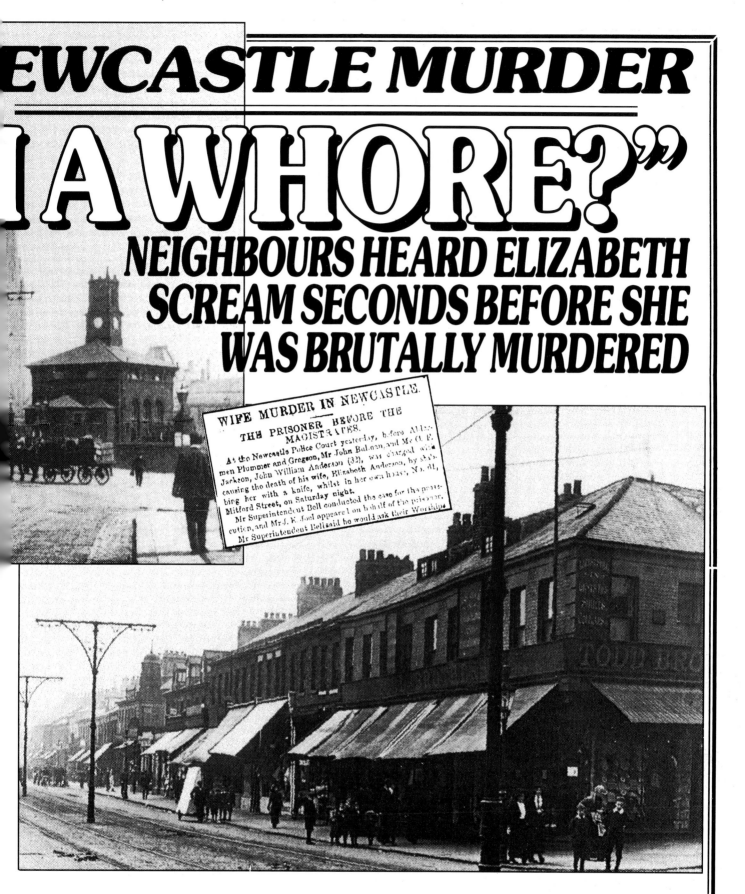

WIFE MURDER IN NEWCASTLE.
THE PRISONER BEFORE THE MAGISTRATES.

At the Newcastle Police Court yesterday, before Aldermen Plummer and Gregson, Mr John Balcomb, and Mr G. F. Jackson, John William Anderson (32), was charged with causing the death of his wife, Elizabeth Anderson, by stabbing her with a knife, whilst in her own house, No. 81, Mitford Street, on Saturday night.

Mr Superintendent Bell conducted the case for the prosecution, and Mr J. E. Joel appeared on behalf of the prisoner. Mr Superintendent Bell said he would ask their Worships

she wouldn't go for him, but she would for Benjamin. Anderson replied that he didn't care who she went for so long as she went. But first he would help her lock up the shop.

Minutes later Ann Purdy looked out of her window at 78 Mitford Street, opposite the Andersons' shop. She saw Elizabeth sitting on the window-sill by the shop, her son standing at her side. Anderson, the neighbour could dimly see, had

entered the darkened shop.

Mrs. Purdy was then surprised to see Elizabeth suddenly rise and run down the street to the home of her friend Mrs. Hope. Anderson emerged from the shop, set off in pursuit and caught his wife as she reached Mrs. Hope's back door. Grabbing her round the waist, he half-carried, half-dragged her back to the shop, young William Anderson trailing behind at a safe distance.

As the boy's parents disappeared into the shop, Anderson slamming and locking the door behind him, William remained in the middle of the road, watching.

The Danskins, hearing the door slam, gave each other a meaningful look.

"Maybe Elizabeth won't go for his beer," said Benjamin.

Putting a finger to her lips, Bridget

motioned to her husband to be quiet so that she could hear what was said. She heard Elizabeth shout, "You won't lock the boy out," adding that if Anderson did so she would go outside and join William.

"No, you won't go out tonight," Anderson replied.

"I will!" his wife answered.

Meanwhile another neighbour attracted by the commotion made her way to Mrs. Purdy's. As she arrived she heard Elizabeth shout, "Let the door be opened ... let my son come in!"

On December 22nd, 1875, John William Anderson became the first person to be hanged *inside* Newcastle Prison — previous executions had all taken place outside the gaol

The shop door opened. Anderson stepped out, saw his son in the road and made a lunge for him. William backed away, turned and ran to where Mrs. Purdy was standing and began to cry.

Anderson looked across for a moment and then returned to the shop ... but not before two more neighbours, Emily Anderson and Isabel English, arrived.

"What youse listening at?" Anderson shouted, disappearing into the shop and slamming the door behind him.

Mrs. Purdy crossed the street to the shop door and listened at the key-hole, while Emily Anderson went to the shop window to see if she could see anything.

After a few seconds' silence they heard a noise as if someone had been slapped. Then they heard Anderson shout, "You bastard! You hit me again and I'll stab you!"

"Am I a whore?" cried Elizabeth.

"No. You are a dirty woman!" her husband replied.

There was another silence, and then the eavesdroppers heard a shuffling sound, as if something were being dragged across the floor. Seconds later there were two blood-curdling screams.

These brought the Danskins running. They arrived to see Anderson dash out of the shop and then slow to a walk, making off down Mitford Street towards Scotswood Road.

Other neighbours were now at the scene. Seeing that the bottom half of the shop door was ajar, Ralph Taylor stepped inside, followed by Benjamin Danskin, who struck a match.

Taylor made his way behind the counter, where he found Elizabeth Anderson lying on her back on the floor. A pool of blood was forming, and when he raised her head and asked if she was all right there was no reply. Elizabeth's eyes opened for a split second and then she lost consciousness.

By her body Taylor found a large knife of the type used by butchers. It was covered with blood to the hilt. Taylor picked it up and showed it to Danskin.

Meanwhile at Laurel Street police station Sergeant William Kennedy and Constable John Dixon were on duty when Anderson walked in and strode to the counter.

"Do you see that?" he asked, holding out his right hand.

The policemen saw that Anderson's palm had been cut. "I have got stabbed," he told them.

"Who has stabbed you?" asked the sergeant.

"I did it myself," said Anderson. "I have committed murder. I have stabbed my wife to death."

Then the door burst open and Benjamin Danskin rushed in, stopping in surprise as he saw his friend. He too had come to report the murder. He confirmed Anderson's story, and his friend then asked him to shake him by the hand. Danskin was happy to oblige, but the sergeant said it "wouldn't do."

"Is she dead?" Anderson asked repeatedly.

"Yes," Danskin told him.

After placing Anderson in a cell the policemen accompanied Danskin to the shop, where Sergeant Kennedy felt Elizabeth Anderson's pulse. It was weak but perceptible. He told Bridget Danskin to fetch Dr. May from Eldon Square. Ten minutes before the doctor arrived, however, Elizabeth Anderson made a gurgling sound and died.

Ralph Taylor handed the sergeant the knife, and back at the police station Anderson told the officer: "The knife I stabbed her with is the same one that she struck me with."

At an inquest on Elizabeth Anderson the following day Sarah Dodd told the coroner that she was passing the Andersons' shop on her way to her home in Tyneside Terrace when she heard a woman scream.

She tried to look through the windows but could see nothing. Then she tried the door, but found it was locked. As she stood outside wondering what to do, the bottom half of the shop door opened and Anderson ducked out.

Grabbing him, she shouted: "Oh, you villain! What have you done?"

Pushing her aside, he said, "I have finished her."

Then he started to run, but soon slowed to a walk as he went away up the street.

The jury returned a verdict of wilful murder against John William

Anderson, and when he appeared before magistrates the following day the court was told by Elizabeth's father that she had not been drinking heavily on the night of her death. He had seen her only an hour before she was murdered, he said, and his daughter had then been quite sober.

Dr. May told the court that Elizabeth had been stabbed four times in the back and three times in her left side. She had also received a cut on her left shoulder. The fatal wound, six inches deep, was large enough for him to insert two fingers.

Above, the rear of terraced houses in Mitford Street, Elswick, and the entrance to a covered yard (far right). The corpse of Elizabeth Anderson was found behind the counter of her shop on Mitford Street by the lodger. Right, William Marwood, John Anderson's executioner

It had passed through her fourth rib, penetrating her lung and her heart.

Shown the knife found beside the body, he said that it could have caused the victim's wounds. He had also examined and stitched Anderson's hand-wound. Asked if this could have been caused by Anderson trying to take the knife from his wife, the doctor said this was possible but improbable.

At Newcastle Assizes on December 1st, 1875, Anderson pleaded "not guilty" when charged with his wife's murder, his counsel striving to have the charge reduced to manslaughter on the grounds of provocation.

If Elizabeth Anderson had not struck her husband first, argued Mr. Skidmore defending, the prisoner would not have lost his self-control and stabbed her.

This defence seemed to have some effect on the jury. After retiring for half an hour they asked the bailiff to inform the judge, Mr. Justice Denman, that they needed pen, ink and paper.

This annoyed the judge, who ordered the jury to be brought back before him. Such a request for writing materials had never been made before, he told them, and he

she attacked me, and unfortunately in a frenzy of madness I committed this rash act.

"I do not ask you, my Lord, to endorse the recommendation of the jury for mercy. It would be a misery for me to continue my life in this world. But yet at the same time if you endorse that recommendation, and if that is granted by my Queen, then I will accept it — but simply on this ground: that it will in some measure do away with the slur cast upon my children's name and in some measure

EXECUTION
OF
JOHN WM. ANDERSON,
FOR THE
MURDER OF HIS WIFE,
IN
MITFORD STREET, NEWCASTLE.

This morning, at eight o'clock, John Wm. Anderson, who was tried and convicted at the last Winter Gaol Delivery for this town for the murder of his wife, Elizabeth Anderson, at No. 61, Mitford Street, in this town, suffered the last penalty of the law by being hanged by the neck until he was dead, within the gaol of this town, where he has been imprisoned since his trial and condemnation before Mr Justice Denman, in the beginning of the present month.

do away with the grief and anguish of my mother and friends."

Sentencing him to death, the judge assured him that while he would forward the jury's recommendation to the proper quarters, Anderson must "not entertain the slightest hope that by word or act of mine in any way shall I attempt to influence the minds of those who will have to deal with the question."

There was no reprieve, and on December 22nd, 1875, John William Anderson became the first person to be hanged inside Newcastle Prison — previous hangings had taken place outside, but a new law now prohibited public executions.

Coincidentally, on the night of Elizabeth Anderson's murder a similar scene had taken place only a mile away. William Carr, a 32-year-old alcoholic like Anderson, had stabbed his wife — who ran a grocery, like Elizabeth Anderson. The same type of knife had been used in each stabbing.

Carr and Anderson knew each other, but there the similarity between their cases ended. Carr's wife was stabbed only in the wrist — police rescued her on hearing her cries for help. And while Anderson went to the scaffold, Carr received only 12 months' imprisonment.

ARRIVAL OF THE EXECUTIONER.

...wood, the executioner, arrived in Newcastle last night ...London, from whence he had travelled by express ...immediately after performing his office in the case of ...at malefactor Henry Wainwright at Newgate prison ...y morning. Marwood, on his arrival, proceeded ...o the prison where he was favoured with lodgings

wasn't going to set a precedent now. But he would be happy to explain the law regarding murder and manslaughter more fully.

"We are scarcely agreed, my Lord," said the jury's foreman.

"Don't tell me any of that," replied Mr. Justice Denman.

The jury retired again, returning half an hour later to find Anderson guilty of murder, but to add a strong recommendation for mercy.

"I suppose," said the judge, "the recommendation is based on the grounds that you think he had some provocation."

"Yes," replied the foreman, "and on account of the apparent unpremeditated nature of the attack."

Asked if he had anything to say before he was sentenced, Anderson surprised the court by appearing at first to reject the jury's recommendation.

Referring to Elizabeth, he said: "She was my wife and I loved her ... I wished to keep her in the house, and

THE GATESHEAD "I MEANT TO

Annie and Craig met originally in 1903 at Barnard Castle (above and top left) where she lived with her mother and sister

SITTING IN his cell at Portland Prison, Thomas Craig read every word of the brief letter over and over again. Dated December 19th, 1909, it was from Winifred, the sister of his 23-year-old girl friend Annie Finn.

"Dear Tommy," it said, "Annie cannot answer any of your letters, and she has told me to tell you not to write to her again. She is soon to be married, and can now have nothing more to do with you."

He had met Annie in 1903, while doing his militia training at Barnard Castle, County Durham, where she lived with her mother and sister. Although he was possessively jealous, Annie had continued to go out with him.

Their romance even survived his arrest the following year for housebreaking and causing grievous bodily harm. On bail pending his trial, he had gone to see Annie to ask her to wait for him, and she had agreed to do so.

Then he was jailed for seven years, but they had corresponded until recently, when Annie's letters had become less frequent. And now, it seemed, they had stopped altogether.

For four years he had thought of little else than seeing her again. Now, in spelling and grammar all his own, he wrote again to Annie.

He had received her sister's letter "very cool," he told her.

"I still love you and will love you true to death, as you should be to me … I will give a few pounds of my pocket to get to no ware you are …

"You will find out as I am not going to stand any more of you Annie, as you no if you are a true woman what a promise means as it is only last August sinse you said 'Keep your heart up, Tom, till we meat.'

"But no one will have you, you will see with sorrow when I come, as you will go ware your mother is … you will be like her in a few weeks time …"

Annie's mother was dead.

"I will be very hot when I meat you so sudden you will think I have been living among mustard, pepper and cloves," Craig's letter continued. "Your happiness will be a short one you will find that I am going to pull the cassel

HOME SECRETARY WINSTON CHURCHILL WAS QUIZZED ON LACK OF POLICE PROTECTION FOR COUPLE IN DANGER

MURDER KILL ANNIE"

VENGEANCE — BUT OVER 5,000 IN HIS D A PETITION FOR HIS REPRIEVE

[castle] down I will brake up the little place for you, as I will be burning when I see it I will be clean made, I will be in a frenzy, I will test my strength against the chap who has robbed me of my love and happiness …

"I will forgive you if you are still Annie Finn," the letter concluded, *"but if you are not well its God help you strate, and to your mother you will go like a flash."*

On his release from prison on March 24th, 1910, after serving five years, Craig went straight to Darlington. Walking into the police station at 3 a.m., he said that he had just been released from jail and had nowhere to go. The duty sergeant directed him to a place that would lodge him for the night.

The next day he made his way to Barnard Castle, to the home of Annie's sister. She refused to tell him where Annie was, saying only that Annie had been married the previous month and

Seven weeks before this man was released from Portland Prison, Annie Finn married somebody else …

wanted to be left alone.

"I know she is in Newcastle," said Craig, now weeping, "and I will search Gateshead and Newcastle until I find her."

He was wasting his time, Winifred told him, saying that she doubted if Annie would talk to him.

"She knows what to expect if she will not speak to me," Craig replied. "If I meet her husband first she will have no husband to go to."

"Look here, Tommy," said Winifred, "I have had plenty of trouble these last five years; we'll have no more."

"I don't think I will do anything, Winnie," Craig replied, saying he was going to catch a train to Darlington.

On the following day he went to Crook, where he found Annie's brother-in-law, Thomas Priestman, working at his job as a carter. Priestman couldn't tell him where

"Keep the doors locked when I am out of the house," he instructed his bride

Soon after the shooting, Craig hurried away to Jarrow

"If I meet her husband first she will have no husband to go to!"

Annie was living but took him to a man who knew her address in Gateshead, which Craig noted on the back of an envelope.

"If I had known of the game that was going on I would have twisted his neck," he said of Annie's husband, 22-year-old Thomas Henderson.

He was now going straight to Gateshead, he told Priestman and the other man, who both asked him to write to them when he had sorted out his affairs.

"I may never get the chance to write again," Craig replied.

He then went to Newcastle, calling at Pape's the gunsmiths, where he bought a revolver and bullets, giving

Why had she thrown him over? "Because I love my husband better than you," Annie told Craig without any hesitation

the impression that he was a householder who wanted to protect his property and signing for the gun and ammunition as "John Wilson, 1 North Road, Durham."

In Gateshead that afternoon he approached a labourer, William Tait, asking him if he knew where the Hendersons lived.

"What Henderson?" asked Tait.

"Tommy Henderson, him that works in the glasshouse," Craig told him.

Then, seeing a police sergeant approaching with a constable, he asked Tait to get in front of him, saying he did not want the police to see him. "I got pinched this morning for gambling," he explained, stepping into a brewery yard until the policeman had passed.

Tait said he knew Henderson and took Craig to the house where he believed he lived.

Shortly before 4 p.m. Thomas Henderson's widowed mother, Mrs. Mary Jane Henderson, answered Craig's knock at her door. When he asked to speak to Annie, Mrs. Henderson asked him if he was a friend. Craig said he was Annie's cousin.

Mrs. Henderson asked him to wait while she fetched her coat. Then she took him to Carter's Yard nearby, where Annie and her husband had set up home at 60 Oakwellgate.

Annie was busy baking and didn't look up as her mother-in-law entered. Thinking her companion was the new insurance man, she told him to sit on a chair in the kitchen, by the door. Mrs. Henderson went into one of the bedrooms, thinking the two might have things to say in private as they were related.

Finishing putting her scones in the oven, Annie now looked up. "You're Tommy Craig, aren't you?" she said. Her husband, who was standing on a chair to hang a picture, turned to see the visitor.

"Yes," said Craig. "And you're Annie Finn."

"I am Mrs. Henderson now," Annie replied, "and this is my husband." Then, referring to Craig's time in prison, she told him, "You don't look much worse for it."

Her husband came across the room, extending his hand to shake Craig's, but the caller ignored him. Instead he asked Annie why she had thrown him over.

"Because I love my husband better than you," she said. Meanwhile Henderson resumed putting up the picture.

Then she heard a shot and her husband cried out and staggered into the scullery. Craig had now turned to

Henderson lay dying with a bullet in his back. As for Annie, she collapsed in the street, later to learn of her husband's death

face her, and she saw a flame come from his gun as a sharp pain seared her left breast. She then heard another shot, and later learned that the bullet had ricocheted off her corsets sparing her further injury.

Craig next ran into the scullery and she heard more shots as she staggered after him to help her husband.

At the same time Mrs. Henderson, hearing the shots, came back into the room to be confronted by Craig pointing a smoking revolver at her.

"Oh, God! Spare me!" she cried.

Craig, his finger wrapped around the trigger, looked at her for a second, lowered the revolver, stuffed it in his pocket and ran from the house.

Annie had already rushed outside and was standing in the street when Craig came out and pushed past her.

He had been pursued by Thomas Henderson, who was found lying in a pool of blood in the high street. Taken to Gateshead police station, Henderson was seen there by Dr. West, the police surgeon, at about 4.10 p.m. He had a bullet in his back,

Chronicle Office, 4 p.m.

THE GATESHEAD MURDER.

CRAIG TRIED TO-DAY AT THE DURHAM ASSIZES.

SENTENCE OF DEATH PASSED.

JURY RECOMMEND PRISONER TO MERCY.

At Durham Assizes, this morning, before Mr. Justice Grantham, Thomas Crake, alias Craig, 24, miner and mechanic, was indicted for the wilful murder of Thomas William Henderson, at Gateshead, on March 26. Mr. Bruce Williamson and Mr. Willoughby Jardine were for the prosecution, and Mr. Griffith Jones defended.

Great interest was manifested in the trial, and the court was crowded before the proceedings commenced. There was a large number of women in the public gallery. The prisoner, a fresh-coloured man, walked firmly into the dock when the case was called, though he showed considerable concern. In answer to the charge he pleaded "Not guilty" in a firm voice. During the trial he occupied a chair in the dock and four warders stood round him.

which had splintered two ribs and torn through a lung, and he died 20 minutes later.

Annie had collapsed in the street and was taken by ambulance to Newcastle Royal Infirmary, where a bullet was removed from her left breast.

Soon on the scene, Detective Inspector Ogle found two bullets in the scullery wall, and a spent cartridge outside on the route Craig had taken to make his escape. A police description of the wanted man stated him to be 24, sturdily built, of "soldierly bearing" and 5 feet $5\frac{1}{2}$ inches tall. Although his real name

Despite his recent experience of prison, Craig did not know how to behave there, and created a lot of trouble ...

was Crake, it was as Craig that he was commonly known.

By the following Wednesday, March 30th, Annie had recovered sufficiently to give evidence at her husband's inquest. Between sobs she told how she had written to Craig for four years, and had then met Thomas Henderson in September, 1909, marrying him in the following February.

Asked by the coroner if she had told her husband of Craig's threatening letter, she said she had done so after they were married. He had told her to put it away and to keep the doors locked when he was not at home. But neither of them had

THE GATESHEAD MURDER.

CRAIG EXECUTED AT DURHAM.

The final scene in the Gateshead murder was enacted, this morning, in Durham Gaol, when judgment of death was executed according to the law upon the young miner, Thomas Craig, or Crake, who forfeited his life for the wilful murder of Thomas William Henderson, at Gateshead, on the 26th of March last, and added his name to the long roll of those who have suffered on the scaffold at Durham. Incidentally it may be of interest to mention that, since the first private execution at Durham in 1869, Craig was the thirty-fourth murderer to be hanged within the prison, and the thirteenth to be executed on the new drop.

THE STORY OF THE CRIME.

The history of the murder can be t

The jury plainly thought that Annie's change of heart about marrying Craig was a mitigating factor in the murder

Durham Cathedral. It was in this city that Craig forfeited his life on the gallows in July 1910; the 34th hanging within Durham Gaol since 1869

thought Craig would carry out his threats.

The coroner then adjourned the inquest for two weeks to give the police time to find Thomas Craig, he said, dead or alive.

Meanwhile Craig had made for Jarrow, but on being seen by a man who questioned him he doubled back towards Chester-le-Street, passed through Gateshead again and made for Ravensworth Woods.

Forty police officers searched those woods on April 12th after receiving reports that a stranger had been seen lurking there, but no one was found. Two days later a farm labourer handed them a note which he had found on the woods' outskirts while on his way to work.

Signed by Craig, the note said that by the time it was found the writer's dead body would be in the woods. A further search was carried out, but there was no sign of Craig.

Meanwhile two burglaries had been reported in the neighbourhood one at Mafferton Farm, the other at Dilston Hall, Corbridge. Food and liquor had been taken in both instances, and Northumberland police believed Craig was

The court heard that Craig had also intended to kill the judge who had originally sentenced him to seven years imprisonment

responsible.

Suspecting that the fugitive was hiding in the area of the Dilston burglary, six Gateshead policemen set out for Corbridge at 7.15 a.m. on April 16th. On arrival they were joined by Northumberland officers and began their search.

At first nothing was found. Then, at the suggestion of a local constable, they began to search the byre, hay loft and other outbuildings at Dilston Cottage Farm. An officer went to the hay loft, and called out: "There's a bag here."

"There's no bag, just hay," said the farmer, who was with other officers in the byre below.

"Then it's a man," said the constable, shifting hay to reveal a man sleeping. On being woken, the man appeared to have been sleeping off the effects of drink. The constable handcuffed him and led him down to his colleagues.

Sergeant Hall, leading the search party, asked the man if he was Thomas Craig.

"Yes," he replied.

Told that he was being arrested, to be taken to Gateshead and charged with the murder of Thomas Henderson, Craig said, "That's right. I didn't mean to kill him, I only meant to wing him. But I meant to kill Annie."

A revolver loaded with five bullets was found in one of his pockets. In his inside coat pocket were numerous letters and photographs, together with five shillings and twopence. Items taken in the burglaries were found scattered around the hay loft. They included a bottle of brandy, a bottle of whisky, some bottles of beer,

He held up the gun so that everyone could see it — and the magistrate's clerk cried out, "Here, put down that weapon ..."

cakes, cigarettes and two overcoats.

News of Craig's capture reached Gateshead before his arrival, and people lined the route from the High Level Bridge to Gateshead police station to catch a glimpse of the fugitive. They were not disappointed. Escorted by four policemen, a dishevelled Craig duly arrived in a taxi.

On April 18th his first court appearance following the shooting was to bring traffic in Swinburne Street to a standstill as crowds sought to catch sight of the prisoner. Charged with the wilful murder of Thomas Henderson and with causing grievous bodily harm to Annie Henderson with intent to murder her, Thomas Craig was remanded in custody, following a court scene which prompted even the accused man to smile.

The revolver found in Craig's possession, Sergeant Hall told the magistrates, was known to be the one used in the Henderson shooting.

Then, as the sergeant held out the gun to enable the bench to see it better, the magistrates' clerk cried, "Here, put down that weapon — it's rather dangerous to point it like that!"

"Oh, it's all right," the sergeant assured him. "It's quite empty now, sir."

Taken to Durham Prison, Craig turned out to be less than a model inmate. He caused so much trouble that he was put in solitary confinement, and four warders guarded him in the dock when his trial at Durham Assizes followed on June 25th. The Crown proceeded only with the murder charge, to which he pleaded "Not guilty" in a firm voice.

Mr. Bruce Williamson, prosecuting, told the court that the case was remarkable for the calculated determination with which the murder had been carried out.

On being charged Craig had said, "I did not intend to kill the man. I intended to kill Annie and then myself, and the reason I did not kill myself was because I did not see Annie drop."

This, coupled with Craig's threatening letter, said Mr. Williamson, proved that Craig had set out to commit murder.

Annie Henderson told the court that Craig was a miner whom she had known for seven years and had intended to marry. While he was in prison she had written to him regularly, telling him she would wait for him until he came out. But in September she had changed her mind.

She said that after Craig had called at her home following his release from prison she had been sitting on a sofa with her back to him when there was a pistol shot. Her husband had jumped down from the chair on which he had been standing. He had cried out, "Oh, Annie!" and had made for the door.

Craig had then pointed his revolver at her and fired, and she felt she had been hit in the breast. The room was then full of smoke, and although more shots were fired she did not feel as if she had been struck again.

From Sergeant Hall the court heard that when Craig was charged he had said he had also intended to shoot Mr. Justice Darling, who had earlier sentenced him to seven years penal servitude. But he had been unable to find out where the judge lived.

Mr. Griffith Jones, defending, called to the witness box Craig's father, who said that in the year his son was born Mrs. Craig had not been right in her mind.

Seeking a verdict of manslaughter,

Annie had been given police protection — until she moved to Gateshead with her new husband. She had not told Gateshead police of the threat

Mr. Griffith Jones told the jury that the provocation of being thrown over by his girl friend had seriously affected Craig's weak mind, after he had for four years been buoyed up by her love and her constant promise to marry him.

But in his summing-up Mr. Justice Grantham told the jury that it would be lamentable if anyone could take the law into their own hands simply because he was annoyed at being jailed or because a judge had given him a long term of imprisonment.

There was no evidence that there was anything wrong with Craig's mind. He appeared to be as sane as anyone else. And there could be no man in the world more determined than Craig had shown himself to be in committing his crime.

After a retirement of 45 minutes the jury returned to find Thomas Craig guilty of Thomas Henderson's murder, but added a recommendation for mercy.

Asked if he had anything to say before he was sentenced, Craig replied, "I have nothing to say, sir. I am quite willing to face death, sir."

The jury had reached the only possible verdict, said the judge, donning the black cap and sentencing Thomas Craig to death.

Execution was scheduled for July 12th, 1910. Meanwhile Craig's friends in his home town of Spennymoor gathered more than 5,000 signatures in their petition for a reprieve, pointing out that the jury had recommended mercy. But on July 8th word came that the Home Secretary could find no grounds for commuting the sentence, and on the appointed day the executioners made their final adjustments to the seven-foot drop that awaited the prisoner.

The execution took less than a minute, and after hanging for the regulation hour Thomas Craig was cut down, the prison surgeon confirming that his death had been instantaneous. But that wasn't quite the end of his story.

There had been a public outcry when the threatening letter he had sent to Annie from Portland Prison was made public. Why hadn't the prison governor stopped the letter? Why hadn't Annie been given police protection on Craig's release? Winston Churchill, the Home Secretary, was asked for an explanation.

It transpired that the prison governor had sent the letter to County Durham's chief constable, and Annie had been duly warned of the letter's contents by an officer of the county police. But on marrying Thomas Henderson and moving to Gateshead, Annie had not informed Gateshead police of the letter and they knew nothing of it until her husband had been murdered.

"The Secretary of State is satisfied that the letter was sent by the governor in order that the police and Miss Finn might be on their guard re Craig," said the official explanation. "As far as the police are aware, the object was defeated by Miss Finn's removal to another police jurisdiction."

But even if Annie and her husband had remained in County Durham with police protection, would the couple have been safe from a killer as determined as Thomas Craig?